Business Communication Strategies

◆

in the

International Business World

Acknowledgement

I would like to thank David and Peggy Dustin Kehe for their innovative "strategies" approach that I have used in the student textbook. Having used their *Conversation Strategies*, I saw an immediate application to the business English course that I teach. With their permission, I proceeded to develop the manuscript that became *Business Communication Strategies*. Thanks, David and Peggy.

– Scott Smith

Other
Pro Lingua Associates
conversation books

Basic Conversation Strategies
Conversation Strategies
Discussion Strategies
Cultural Differences

Faces
Ask and Task
Conversation Inspirations
Improvisations
Surveys for Conversation
In My Opinion

Basic Dictations
Great Dictations
Interactive Dictations
Dictations for Discussion

www.ProLinguaAssociates.com

Business Communication Strategies

in the International Business World

Scott Smith

PRO LINGUA  ASSOCIATES

Pro Lingua Associates, Publishers
74 Cotton Mill Hill, Suite A314
Brattleboro, Vermont 05301 USA
Office: 802-257-7779
Orders: 800-366-4775
Email: info@ProLinguaAssociates.com
WebStore: www.ProLinguaAssociates.com
SAN: 216-0579

*At Pro Lingua
our objective is to foster an approach
to learning and teaching that we call
interplay, the interaction of language
learners and teachers with their materials,
with the language and culture,
and with each other in active, creative,
and productive play.*

ISBN 13: 978-0-86647-306-4 • 10: 0-86647-306-8

This book was designed and set in type by Arthur A. Burrows. Adobe *Century Schoolbook* is the type face used for both text and display. It is a digital adaptation of one of the most popular faces of the 20th Century. Century's distinctive roman and italic fonts and its clear, dark strokes and serifs were designed, as the name suggests, to make schoolbooks easy to read. The original, elegant type was cut in 1924 by Morris Fuller Benton for the American Type Foundry of Elizabeth, New Jersey, the largest and one of the most distinguished type foundries in the United States from 1892 to 1993. It was adapted by Monotype in 1928, and since then many "Century" and "Schoolbook" faces have been developed, as typesetting and printing technology have evolved from Linotype and film to digital type.

The photographs illustrating this book are from Dreamstime.com Agency: p. iv © Ron Chapple Studios, p. xi © Nruboc/Stephen Coburn, p. 1 © Dmitriy Shironosov, p. 12 © Christophe.rolland1, p.27 © Gilaxia, p 29 © Ron Chapple Studios, p. 40 © 477344sean, p. 42 top © Galina Barskaya, p. 42 bottom © Karen Roach, p. 54 © Eastwest Imaging, p. 63 © Yuri Arcurs, p. 69 © Monkey Business Images, p. 74 © Dragan Trifunovic, p. 79 © Carroteater, p. 83 © Andres Rodriguez, p. 93 © Marcin Balcerzak, p.104 © Corpix, p.113 © Scott Maxwell, p. 114 © Markhunt, p. 122 © Nina Schnapp, p. 130 © Auremar, p. 136 © Michael Pettigrew, p. 141 © Orange Line Media, p. 145 © Dallaeventsinc, p. 149 © Jonathan Ross, p. 155 © Yuri Arcurs, p. 165 © Photoeuphoria, p. 174 © Pavel Yazykov, p. 183 © Marcin Balcerzak, p. 193 © Monkey Business Images, p. 209 © Ron Chapple Studios, p. 210 © Franz Pflueg, p. 211 © Hongqi Zhang, p. 214 © Drizzd, p. 224 © Shuttlecock, p. 235 © Erwin Purnomo. The cover design is by A.A. Burrows using photos © by Jiang Daohua (front), Jonathan Ross (back), and Konstantin Remizov (background). The book was printed and bound by Gasch Printing in Odenton, Maryland.

Printed in the United States of America.
Fourth printing 2017

◆ Contents ◆

◆ Introduction ◆

This is an intermediate-level textbook with accompanying listening material on CD for students who already have a working knowledge of English. The emphasis is on oral communication, and the goal is to prepare students for the linguistic challenges (especially speaking and listening skills) they will face in the international business world, both on and off the job. While most students will have had some work experience to draw on, those without it can imagine their dream job – company and position – and take on that role throughout the book.

The four sections of each unit are designed to maximize speaking time for students and to minimize teacher talk. It is recommended that the sequence of the units and the sections be followed carefully for maximum effectiveness. Doing so will minimize planning time and the need for supplementary materials.

The book is designed to be effective with two people (teacher and student) as well as with medium-size and large classes.

Section 1 – Starting Point (Warm Up)

To get the students communicating immediately, each unit starts with a warm up – questions that stimulate conversation about the topic of the unit. Typically, they are pair exercises that relate to the communicative function of the unit (Getting Acquainted, Making Small Talk, *etc*.). This leads into group work, and then into a class discussion (both of which can easily be done as pair work if only two people are using the book).

Section 2 – Communication Strategies

This section is the core of the unit, where the strategies are introduced and practiced.

Part 1 begins with a presentation of phrases that are commonly used in the context of the unit's topic. This part is also available on the CDs for listening and pronunciation practice. **Part 2** is a controlled practice in which the students use the phrases to complete the dialogs by filling in the blanks. **Part 3** is a conversational flow chart, which the students follow in a guided conversation. After the flow chart, the activities will vary, depending on the focus of the unit. The emphasis here is on moving from controlled practice (internalizing the language) to free practice (using it fluently). As the students progress through the book, previous strategies will be recycled in this section, as well as in Section 4 (Activity). This recycling helps the students strengthen their use of previously introduced strategies and also gives them opportunities to employ a variety of strategies within each topic area.

Section 3 – Reading

This section features a reading that is about the focus of the unit. It also introduces new vocabulary, idioms, and expressions, as well as vocabulary strategies and some simple reading strategies to check comprehension (*e.g.,* main idea, summarizing, *etc.*). In addition, the business communication strategies will be incorporated into the activities in this section.

The section begins by activating students' background knowledge. This is followed by a discussion, reading preview, and some vocabulary building. All four of these activities help students better understand the reading. After the article, there is a comprehension check and another discussion.

Section 4 – Activity

This section helps students consolidate and apply the knowledge and skills they learned in the unit. It is the most detailed and challenging part of the unit, but the students should be well prepared for it after working through the previous three sections. The activity will differ from unit to unit depending on the focus of the unit.

Teacher's Guide with Answers

A separate Teacher's Guide includes:
1. **Teaching tips** to help make the implementation of the material effective, and
2. **Answers** to all the Communication Strategies dialogs and other activities.
The **Business Terms** used in this book are listed on pages 241 to 243. They are also available in the Teacher's Guide on photocopyable pages for making **vocabulary cards**.
• Note that if you plan to read the Communication Strategies dialogs to your students, the complete script in the Teacher's Guide will make your reading easier.

Business Communication Strategies

in the International Business World

◆ Getting Acquainted ◆

Section 1 ◆ Starting Point: Meeting new people

A. Warm Up: Get to know your classmates.

Part 1: What does "appropriate" mean? What is the appropriate way to greet someone in your culture? What would be inappropriate?

Part 2: Appropriately greet and introduce yourself to your classmates. Include the following information:

       ◆ Your full name
       ◆ The name you want your classmates to call you
       ◆ Your company (or school)
       ◆ Your job title (or major and year)

B. Group Work: Discuss the following questions in small groups.

What does "first impression" mean? How important are first impressions? How much do they really matter?

How do the following factors influence your first impression of someone?

Gender	Occupation
Race	Physical attractiveness
Nationality	Expressiveness and charisma
Language	Fashion and style
Culture	Others (if any): _____

Which of these factors influences you the most? Why?
What is your self-concept (*i.e.* your impression of yourself)?
Do you think people see you differently from the way you see yourself?
Does this ever cause people to get the wrong first impression of you?
Have you ever gotten the wrong first impression of someone else? Explain.

C. As a Class:

In a business context, which of the following personal and career information is appropriate to give when you meet someone for the first time? Put a ✔ next to what is appropriate and an ✘ next to what is not.

✘ Age	✘ Political orientation
✘ Height and weight	✔ Religious beliefs
✘ Marital and family status	✔ Hobbies and interests
✔ Educational background	✘ Personal issues
✔ Company and job details	✔ Future plans
✔ Salary	✔ Contact information

Can you think of any other information that would be inappropriate to ask about or share when you first meet someone? Does this depend on context (*i.e.* the situation and where you are in the world)?

Section 2 ♦ Communication Strategies: ⊙ CD 1 track 1
Greetings and introductions

Part 1: Read, listen to, and say these sentences and phrases.

Greeting and responding

Good morning/afternoon/evening.
How are you?
I'm fine, thanks.

Introducing yourself

My name is _____.   Nice to meet you.
I'm _____.   Nice meeting you.
                               Pleased to meet you.
                               It's a pleasure to meet you.
                               Glad to meet you (too).

Introducing others

I'd like you to meet (my boss) *Ivank* (name).
_____ (name), this is my colleague _____ (name).
Allow me to introduce _____. He's/She's my _____.
_____ (name), have you met _____ (name)?
_____ (name), do you know _____ (name)?
Have you two been introduced?

Asking about someone's job

What do you do?   How long have you been working there?
Who do you work for?   Do you like what you do?
What kind/type of   Have you worked anywhere else?
  company is that?

Giving information about your job

I'm a/an _____.   I manage/supervise _____.
I'm in charge of _____.   I support/assist/help with _____.
I'm responsible for *my studies*   I deal with _____.

Giving information about your company

It's a _____ company.
I've been with the company for _____ months/years.
I used to work at _____.
I worked as a _____.

Part 2: Fill in the blanks with the phrases in **bold** type. When you're finished, read the dialogs with a partner. Then switch roles and read the dialogs again.

⊙ CD 1 track 2

who do you work for **Nice to meet you, too**
Where are you located **How do you do**
I'm in charge of **What do you do for the company**
What kind of company is that **How long**
I've been with the company for

A: Hello. My name is Joyce Livingston.

B: _____. I'm Richard Santiago.

A: Nice to meet you.

B: _____.

A: If you don't mind me asking, _____, Richard?

B: I work for Shorecast.

A: _____?

B: It's a broadcasting company.

A: _____?

B: Our headquarters is in Los Angeles, but I work at our San Francisco office.

A: _____?

B: I'm a camera operator.

A: Really? What do you do exactly?

B: _____ filming the morning news show.

A: Interesting! _____ have you been working there?

B: _____ about ten years now. How about you, Joyce?

What do you do? **how do you two know each other**
It's a pleasure to meet you, too **I'd like you to meet**
have you met

A: Kazu, _____ my new colleague, Isabel?

B: No, not yet.

A: Isabel, _____ a good friend of mine, Kazu Izawa.

C: Hi, pleased to meet you, Kazu.

B: _____, Isabel.

C: So _____?

A: Kazu and I have been friends since college.

Part 3: With a partner, create and practice a dialog based on the following flow chart.

Use business communication strategies from this chapter to help you. When you are finished, switch roles. Create and practice a similar dialog **without** using the flow chart.

A   **B**

A1: Greet your partner and introduce yourself.

B1: Greet your partner and introduce yourself.

A2: Respond to your partner's greeting.

B2: Respond to your partner's greeting.

A3: Ask your partner who she or he works for.

B3: Answer your partner's question.

A4: Ask your partner what kind of company that is.

B4: Answer your partner's question.

A5: Ask your partner where her or his company is located.

B5: Answer your partner's question.

A6: Ask your partner what she or he does for the company.

B6: Answer your partner's question.

A7: Ask your partner for more details about his or her job.

B7: Answer your partner's question.

A8: Ask your partner how long she or he has been working there.

B8: Answer your partner's question.

A9: Ask if your partner likes what she or he does.

B9: Answer your partner's question.

A10: Ask if your partner has worked anywhere else.

B10: Answer your partner's question.

Part 4: Use role play to act out the following situation with different classmates.

You are at a business conference in your city. First, create a role for yourself based on this information. You don't know any of the attendees, but you want to make some contacts in your field. Pretend you are in the lobby after a presentation, and you meet some new people. Find out some or all of the following information about them. Feel free to find out additional information as well.

Name
Where they're from
What company they work for
What they do for the company
Reason they are at the conference
How many times they've attended the conference
Their feelings about the conference location
Where they are staying and how they like it there
Sightseeing plans
When they will return home

Part 5: Practice introducing your classmates to each other. With every introduction, ask questions about each other's job (or school/major).

Section 3 ♦ Reading: First impressions

*Making a good first impression is important for building relationships
with other people, especially people you do business with. With the
following exercises and article, you will have an opportunity to examine
this issue and express your opinions about it.*

A. Activate: Think about a few strangers you have seen today or yesterday.

B. Discuss: Describe some of the people you remember (*i.e.*, the ones who stood out).
What kind of impression did they make on you? Why?

C. Focus: In the box below, write a list of ideas for making a good first impression.

Compare your list to the tips given in the following article.

D. Read: Read the following article.

When it comes to first impressions, perception is often more powerful and
important than reality. Your physical appearance, demeanor, mannerisms,
body language, clothes, and accessories are being evaluated each and every
day by people all around you. These judgments are made in just a few sec-
onds, and many of them will never change.

While these hasty judgments may seem unfair, you can do something to
foster a favorable response. First of all, dress for success. Wear clothes that
are modest and appropriate for the place you'll be going to or event you'll be

attending. In addition, make sure that your clothes are clean and that they fit well. By doing this, you will avoid looking sloppy and let others know that you care about your appearance.

If you have an opportunity to meet someone new, there are a number of things you can do to make a good first impression. Start by smiling, projecting a positive attitude, and being cool. Once the conversation starts, speak clearly with a rate of speech that is easy to follow. Also, be polite and courteous throughout your meeting. Furthermore, use the person's name frequently. This makes the meeting more personal and demonstrates how important you consider them to be.

In addition to presenting yourself in a good light, make sure you're attentive to the other person's needs. The easiest way to do this is let the person you are talking to be the center of attention. This means being a good listener and not talking on and on about yourself (especially about your problems or any concerns and interests you have in your life).

Meeting someone for the first time can be stressful, but try to relax and be yourself. It will be easy for other people to tell if you are showing off or trying to impress them.

E. Comprehension Check: *Without* looking back at the article, how many tips for making a good impression can you remember? List them in the box below.

Now check the article again to see how many you remembered.

F. Rethink: How important is it to make a good first impression? Why?

Section 4 ♦ Activity: **People and the impressions they make**

Directions: With a partner, read the descriptions below and discuss what kind of impression each person would make. Give reasons for your answers.

Person 1

A new colleague of yours is very polite and courteous when you first meet him. He also quickly proves himself to be very helpful around the office and generous with his time. In addition, he is very humorous and a delight to be around in any social situation. You always notice how comfortable and relaxed you feel in his presence.

Person 2

You meet a new business partner who is noisily taking on her cell phone when you are trying to greet one another. She seems to be more interested in her telephone conversation than meeting you. When she finally gets off the phone, she seems distracted. She makes intermittent eye contact, leading you to wonder what she is looking at around you. You never feel that you have her whole attention.

Person 3

Your new boss is good-looking and well-mannered, and dresses for success. When you meet, he gives you a firm handshake and looks you straight in the eye. You notice that he's smiling and in a good mood. He makes you the center of attention and praises the hard work you have done for the company over the years. He tells you that he is available any time you have questions or need assistance with something. He promises to do what he can to make your experience at work the best that it can be.

Person 4

You have been asked to pick up an important client at the airport. From the moment the client steps off the plane, you notice that she is cranky. You blame the long flight until you realize that she is critical about everything: the airlines, the airport, passersby, your city, and the hotel. Her complaints continue the next day at the office and don't stop until you see her off at the airport the following evening.

Person 5

You are on a business trip. One of the executives invites you to dinner. After a long day of meetings, you look forward to relaxing and getting to know one of the people you will be doing business with. When the two of you get together, it is clear from the beginning that he thinks highly of himself. In fact, not only does he boast about himself and his career achievements, he completely dominates the conversation. During the course of the entire evening, you hardly have a chance to say anything.

What advice would you give to the three people who would make an unfavorable impression? How could they have handled each of their situations differently?

♦ Making Small Talk ♦

Section 1 ♦ Starting Point: Being social

A. Warm Up: Discuss the following questions with a partner.

    1. Do you enjoy meeting new people? Why or why not?

    2. Do you think that you have good people skills? Explain.

    3. What does "rapport" mean? What's the best way to build rapport with someone?

B. Group Work:

What does "small talk" mean? In a business context, which of the following are common small-talk topics? Which ones do you tend to avoid talking about? Put a ✔ next to each topic that you would normally talk about with your business associates and an ✘ next to what you would avoid.

___ weather	___ death
___ intimate relationships/sex	___ movies or TV shows
___ sports	___ politics
___ religion	___ clothes and fashion
___ traffic or commuting	___ food
___ weekend activities/plans	___ traveling and vacations
___ personal issues	___ family
___ global warming	___ controversial issues
___ salary	___ hobbies
___ the news/current events	___ hometown
___ health and exercise	

Write one of the topics above next to its corresponding conversation starter below.

Weather It's so cold outside!	_____ It took forever to get to work today.
_____ Did you watch the game last night?	_____ Hey, you're back. How was Shanghai?
_____ What are you up to on Saturday?	_____ Have you seen "The Departed"?
_____ This is delicious!	_____ What do you like to do in your free time?
_____ Nice sweater!	_____ Did you read the paper today?
_____ Where are you from?	_____ Have you been working out?
_____ What do you think about climate change?	_____ Do you have any children?

C. As a Class:

Think of some more conversation starters – statements or questions – for each of the common small-talk topics above.

Section 2 ♦ Communication Strategies: Small-talk expressions

⊙ CD 1 track 3

Part 1: Read, listen to, and say these sentences and phrases.

Rejoinders

Rejoinders tell the person you are talking to that you are listening to them, you understand what they are saying, and you are interested in the conversation. They are very important conversation fillers (i.e. they prevent any awkward silence between speakers).

Um-hm.	Wow!
Uh-huh.	Cool!
Really?/Really!	Oh, no!
I see.	That's too bad.
Oh, yeah?/Yeah?	OK.
That's great.	Right.
You're kidding!	All right.
I can't believe it!	
No way!	

Follow-up questions

Follow-up questions help you get details and talk about a topic more deeply. If you ask someone a question and they answer it, it is often good to ask a question about their answer. These are often used in conjunction with rejoinders to show that you are listening and interested in what the person you are talking to is saying.

Who ___?	Where ___?
What ___?	Why ___?
When ___?	How ___?

Conversation initiators

Start with a greeting and introduction if you do not know the person. If, on the other hand, the two of you have met before, use one of the following expressions.

How're you doing?	What's up?
How's everything?	What's going on?
How's it going?	Can I talk to you for a minute?
How've you been?	Do you have a minute?/Got a minute?

Conversation closers

You'll have to excuse me. I have to ___.
I'd better get going.
I'll let you get back to work.
I won't take (up) any more of your time.
It was good to see you./It was great seeing you.
It was nice talking to you, but I need to get going.

Make plans to keep in touch

I'll be in touch.
I'll give you a call.
I'll see you (again) soon.
Let's get together again soon.

Part 2: Fill in the blanks with the phrases in **bold** type. When you're finished, read the dialogs with a partner. Then switch roles and read the dialogs again.

⊙ CD 1 track 4

Really   Um-hm   how's it   How long   how're you doing

A: Hey, _____ going?

B: Hey, _____?

A: I'm just taking care of a few things before my business trip to Paris tomorrow.

B: Paris? Wow! _____ are you going to be there?

A: About ten days.

B: _____? You'll definitely have time to do some sightseeing.

A: Actually, I'm looking forward to that. You went to Paris last year, right?

B: _____. I had to give a presentation at the management conference.

Can you recommend   I don't want to be rude   I need to get going
I'll see you   Where   I see

[Continued] A: _____ did you stay?

B: I forgot the name of the hotel, but it was in the center of the city, right near all the tourist attractions.

A: _____. _____ some places to see or things to do?

B: You have to see the Eiffel Tower, of course. I'd also check out the Arc de Triomphe and Notre Dame.

A: Great! I'll definitely put those on my list.

B: Hey, _____, but _____. I have a meeting in ten minutes.

A: No problem. _____ when I get back.

B: OK. Have a great time!

I'll give you a call   that's great   What's up
let's get together sometime soon   What   Do you have
When   You're kidding

A: _____ a minute?

B: Sure. _____?

A: I just wanted to let you know that Friday will be my last day.

B: _____! Did you get fired?

A: No! I found another job in Toronto.

B: Oh, _____! _____ will you be doing?

A: I'm going to be an account executive for an advertising agency.

B: Ahh! I remember you telling me that you were going to apply for that job.

A: Yeah! I've really enjoyed working here and with you, but I'm looking forward to doing something different.

B: I see. _____ will you be moving?

A: At the end of the month.

B: Really? Well, _____.

A: That sounds great. _____ in the next couple of days and we'll set something up.

Part 3: With a partner, create and practice a dialog based on the following flow chart.

Use business communication strategies from this chapter to help you. When you are finished, switch roles. Create and practice a similar dialog **without** using the flow chart.

A

A1: Use a conversation initiator.

A2: Tell your partner that you will be going on vacation next week – but **don't** reveal your destination.

A3: Answer your partner's question. (*choose any overseas destination)

A4: Answer your partner's question.

A5: Answer your partner's question.

A6: Answer your partner's question. Now ask if your partner has ever been there before.

A7: Express your excitement about the trip.

A8: Promise to keep in touch while you are away.

A9: Express thanks and say goodbye.

B

B1: Respond to the conversation initiator.

B2: Use a rejoinder and then ask where your partner is going.

B3: Use a rejoinder and ask how long your partner will be gone.

B4: Ask your partner what s/he will do there.

B5: Use a rejoinder and ask your partner who s/he is going on vacation with.

B6: Respond accordingly.

B7: Use a conversation closer.

B8: Respond and tell your partner to have a safe trip.

Part 4: Practice making small talk about something in the news these days. Begin with a conversation starter and use business communication strategies to talk for 3-5 minutes. When you're finished, switch partners and pick a different news item. Try making small talk one more time.

Part 5: Choose any topic and make small talk with your teacher. Engage in a conversation with him or her and try to sustain it for as long as you can. You can do this individually, in groups, or as a class. Repeat as necessary.

Section 3 ♦ Reading: Small-talk tips

Small talk is an essential social skill that can positively or negatively affect careers, friendships, and romances. In the following exercises and article, you will have an opportunity to examine this issue and express your opinions about it.

A. Activate: Discuss the following questions with a partner.

1. Why is small talk important?
2. What do people hope to achieve with small talk?

B. Discuss: Work with your partner and another pair.

Think about any experiences you've had making small talk. When were you the most successful? Describe a situation, to include the place, people, what you talked about, and why it went so well. Now think of a time when things went badly. What happened in that situation?

C. Focus: The following people have a difficult time starting a conversation and making small talk. What advice would you give each one? Help them overcome the obstacle that is blocking their path to potentially meaningful communication.

1. Anne has a fear of being rejected by people she meets for the first time. She does not know how to successfully engage someone in a conversation and feels that she never has anything interesting to say once it begins.

2. Pedro doesn't know how to involve himself in an ongoing conversation. He usually remains quiet and feels increasingly anxious as the conversation goes on. It's common for him to berate himself afterwards for not being able to participate in the way he wanted or hoped to.

3. Masako thinks chitchat is a complete waste of time. She's almost always bored or irritated when she is forced to make small talk. It's common for her to feel a lot of stress and frustration from this type of social encounter.

D. Read: Read the following article.

Although many people do not enjoy small talk, thinking it's silly, boring, or super-ficial, never underestimate how important it can be for business relationships and in your personal life. After all, small talk is how we gather information about and understand other people. It also gives us a chance to make a favorable impression.

Fortunately, starting a conversation and making small talk with confidence are skills that can be learned. Here are some tips to help you do them well:

☞ *Prepare for a function.* Think of three things you want to talk about as well as four generic questions that will get others talking.

☞ *Greet people appropriately and remember their names.* Set a positive and welcoming tone, and make the other person feel important and at ease.

☞ *Focus on them.* People love to talk about themselves. Be careful not to ask too many questions.

☞ *Be a good listener.* By paying attention, you will be able to ask appropriate and intelligent questions to keep the conversation moving.

☞ *Find some common interests.* It's always enjoyable to converse with someone who likes the same things you do.

☞ *Ask open-ended questions.* These require people to express their thoughts or feelings about something.

☞ *Follow the other person's lead.* If interest in the conversation is sustained, keep going. If the person you are talking to is looking at his or her watch or for an escape strategy, then find a way to close the conversation.

☞ *Have a few exit lines ready.* This will make the conversation end successfully.

It also helps to:

☞ *Be informed.* Read newspapers, magazines, and books, watch TV, listen to the radio, and surf the Internet. Note interesting facts, and remember funny stories that you can bring into the conversation.

☞ *Immerse yourself in culture.* Movies, music, sports, fashion, and art are great sources for informal conversation.

☞ *Practice by conversing with people you encounter.* Start a conversation on a daily basis with cashiers, waiters and waitresses, gas station attendants, people you are in line with, people sitting next to you on the bus, train, or subway, and your neighbors.

☞ *Force yourself to get into small-talk situations.* Doctors' waiting rooms, parties, and office meetings are common places. You could also join a club or take a class. In addition to meeting some new people, you'll have a chance to polish your social skills.

☞ *Keep it light.* Talking about politics, religion, or controversial issues is not the best way to make a person feel comfortable in what is supposed to be an informal situation.

☞ *Work on confidence.* Remember, the more you know, the more you know you can talk about.

By practicing these skills until they become second nature you will increase your own self-esteem and learn how to start a conversation easily. Repetition and determination are the key factors. In essence, learning how to start a conversation is really just a process of practicing your social skills until they become a habit.

E. Comprehension Check: A summary is a brief statement that lists the important ideas of a reading in your own words.

Prepare a summary that will help you remember the important information from the reading. Start by making a list of essential points from the article in the box below. Try to write **key words** only.

> prepare for function
> greet people appropriately and remember names
> focus on them

When you are finished, use this list and take turns summarizing what you read with a partner. Then try again without your notes.

F. Rethink: What are the dangers of underestimating the importance of small talk?

Section 4 ◆ Activity: Practice making small talk

Directions: With your classmates, practice making small talk with the topics in
   "Starting Point – Group Work." Begin with a conversation starter, then use
   rejoinders and follow-up questions to keep the conversation flowing for
   3-5 minutes. When the time is up, close the conversation and find a new
   person to make small talk with. Choose different topics and repeat the process
   until you have had a chance to talk to several classmates.

When you are finished, make small talk about your ideal work environment – this
time in small groups. Discuss some or all of the following points:

☞   Type of company
☞   Type of job
☞   Type of boss
☞   Management style
☞   Co-workers

☞   Working hours
☞   Salary
☞   Type of office
☞   Office facilities
☞   Perks and benefits

☞   Atmosphere
☞   Job security
☞   Professional development
☞   Room for advancement
☞   Rewards

♦ Telephoning ♦

Section 1 ♦ Starting Point: Using the telephone

A. Warm Up: Do you know what each of the following telephone terms means? Put a ✔ next to any terms that you **do not** know.

☐ 800 number	☐ hang up
☐ answering machine	☐ IDD/international prefix
☐ area code	☐ keypad
☐ bad connection	☐ local call
☐ busy signal	☐ long distance
☐ call display	☐ not in service
☐ caller ID	☐ operator
☐ conference call	☐ phone book
☐ country code	☐ receiver
☐ dial tone	☐ service charge
☐ directory assistance	☐ speakerphone
☐ disconnect	☐ toll-free
☐ extension	☐ voice mail

Now compare your list with a classmate's. Explain terms that your partner does not know. If necessary, ask your teacher for help.

B. Pair Work: Match the three stages of a telephone call on the left with their corresponding functions or strategies on the right. Write the letters on the lines.

☎ Preparing for the call ____   (A) Ask to speak to someone
                       ____   (B) Say goodbye
                       ____   (C) Be clear about why you are calling
☎ Starting the call   ____   (D) Confirm information
                       ____   (E) Think about what you want to say
                       ____   (F) Use a greeting and introduce yourself
☎ Closing the call   ____   (G) Express appreciation
                       ____   (H) State reason for the call
                       ____   (I) Anticipate any problems you may face

Question: When you take a message for someone, what key information must you be sure to write down?

C. As a Class:

Make a list of problems you might face when speaking English on the telephone at your workplace. Add to the list below.

```
Person talks too fast
Don't understand some of the words
```

How would you handle each of these problems?

Section 2 ◆ Communication Strategies: Telephone talk

⊙ CD 1 track 5

Part 1: Read, listen to, and say these sentences and phrases.

Answering the phone

Hello.
Good morning/afternoon. This is _____.
This is _____. How can I help you?
_____ (first name) speaking.

Introducing yourself

Hello. This is _____ from _____ (your company).
Hello. My name's _____. I'm calling from _____ (your company).
Hi. It's _____ (your name).

Asking to speak with someone

May/Can I speak to ___?
Is ___ in?

Asking who is calling

May/Can I ask who is calling?

Asking what the purpose of the call is

What's it regarding?
May I ask what it's regarding?

Delaying the caller

Please hold./Hold, please.
Just a moment, please.
She's on another line.* Would you like to hold?
Can you hold for a second? I have another call.
I'm busy right now. Can I call you back?
I'll get back to you as soon as I can.

Making arrangements

When would be a good time?
When's good for you?
How about _____ (day)?
What about the _____ (date)?
I'm afraid I can't make it _____ (day).
Something's come up. Can we meet on _____ (day)?

Making special requests

Can you speak up/a little louder, please?
I can't hear you very well. Could you repeat that?
Could you please speak more slowly?
It's a bad connection. Please call me back.
I'm sorry. I didn't catch that/what you said.
Could you spell that, please?

Taking a message

S/he's not in. Can I take a message?
S/he's not available at the moment. May I take a message?
Would you like to leave a message?
Would you like him/her to call you back?
Can I have your number?
If you give me your number, I'll (be sure to) have him/her call you back.

Leaving a message

Could you tell him/her I called?
Could you ask him/her to call me back?
Please tell him/her I'll call back later.
No, that's okay. I'll call back later.

* *Ways to say someone is busy: stepped away from his or her desk, in a meeting, with someone right now, on vacation, on a business trip, or out of the office.*

Part 2: Fill in the blanks with the phrases in **bold** type. When you're finished, read the dialogs with a partner. Then switch roles and read the dialogs again.

⊙ CD 1 track 6

hold   This is   Can I leave a message   How can I help you

on another line   May I speak to

A: Good afternoon. JSX Company. _____ Chris.

_____ ?

B: Hello. This is Mike from Suppliers Limited. _____

Elise Richards, please?

A: She's _____ right now. Would you like to

_____?

B: _____ instead?

It's   at   speaking   meet
I have to reschedule   how about

A: Bob _____ . How can I help you?

B: Hey Bob! _____ Joyce. How are you?

A: Good! I've been meaning to call you.

B: Are we still on for tomorrow night?

A: I'm really sorry, but _____ .

B: That's too bad. I was really looking forward to seeing you.

A: Well, _____ Friday

     _____ 7:00 instead?

B: Sure, no problem. Do you want to _____ at the
same place?

expecting   May I ask who   stepped away   May I speak
Would you like to leave a message   tell her

A: _____ to Ms. Hashimoto please?

B: _____ is calling?

A: My name is Phillip. She's _____ my call.

B: Just a moment please. (Pause) It looks like she _____
from her desk.   _____ ?

A: Just _____ I called.

repeat   Could you spell the name   hear you

A: I couldn't _____ very well. Could you
     _____ that?

B: Please express mail the package to Giovanni Moretti. He's expecting
it tomorrow.

A: _____ , please?

B: Sure. It's G-I-O . . .

Part 3: With a partner, create and practice three dialogs based on the following flow chart. Use business communication strategies from this chapter to help you. When you are finished, switch roles. Create and practice similar dialogs **without** using the flow chart.

Dialog 1

A1: Answer the phone.

B1: Introduce yourself and ask to speak to Mr. Chen.

A2: Ask the caller to hold.

B2: Respond to your partner.

A3: Ask to take a message
– Mr. Chen is not available.

B3: Leave a message

A4: Respond to your partner.

B4: Say thank you and goodbye.

Dialog 2

A1: Answer the phone.

B1: Use a friendly greeting
– you know your partner.

A2: Make small talk.

B2: Make small talk.

A3: Suggest getting together.

B3: Respond positively to idea.

A4: Make arrangements.

B4: Respond to your partner.

A5: Say you look forward to seeing your partner.

B5: Respond to your partner.

A6: Close the call.

B6: Say goodbye.

Dialog 3

A1: Answer the phone.

B1: Introduce yourself – but so that your partner can't understand you.

A2: Make a special request.

B2: Clearly say, "Can you hear me now?"

A3: Respond by saying, "Much better."

B3: Apologize, then introduce yourself again and ask to speak with Ms. Lopez.

A4: Ask your partner to wait
 – Ms. Lopez is on the phone.

        B4: Respond to your partner.

A5: (Pause) Tell your partner
 that Ms. Lopez is still on
 the phone.

        B5: Ask if you can leave a message.

A6: Get your partner's phone number.

        B6: Respond.

A7: Say that you will have
 Ms. Lopez call when she gets
 off the phone.

        B7: Say thank you and goodbye.

Part 4: Without looking back at the communication strategies and practice dialogs, role-play the following situations with a partner. Sit back to back to simulate making an actual telephone call. When you are finished, switch roles and repeat.

Role play 1

One of you calls a very busy office. You want to speak to a business associate who is on another line. As the call is not important, there is no need to leave a message.

Role play 2

You and your partner know each other. Make some small talk. Then make arrangements to get together in spite of your busy schedules.

Role play 3

One of you is calling an office to speak to a colleague who is on a business trip. Although the connection is bad, you need to leave an important message.

Role play 4

As a class, go back to Group Work 2 in Starting Point and act out one or more of the situations you came up with.

Part 5: Does practice make perfect? Assess your business telephoning skills.

 Pairs: Perform one of the role plays in front of the class.

 Class: Observe each pair and take notes. Give feedback. Tell each person what they did well and, if necessary, what they could work on.

Section 3 ◆ Reading: Cell phone etiquette

A. Activate and Discuss:

1. What kind of cell phone do you have?
2. What features does your cell phone have? What features would you like it to have?
3. Would you like an all-in-one device or do you prefer having a simpler phone for telephone calls and text messages only?
4. Are you addicted to your cell phone? Could you live without it?
5. Does it ever bother you when people use their cell phones in public places?

B. Focus: Make a list of cell phone annoyances. Discuss why each one bothers you.

C. Read: Read the following article.

Unquestionably, the cell phone is an essential business tool. What would we do without it? It is hard to imagine, considering our dependency. But as useful as cell phones are, there are some obvious drawbacks. Of these, poor etiquette is the most glaring. Far too many people are inconsiderate of others when they use their cell phones in public. What happened to common courtesy?

To make sure that you do not irritate those around you, particularly people you do business with, follow these universally accepted rules for using a cell phone politely. First of all, spare others your babble. Nobody wants to be subjected to the details of your conversation, no matter how important the call may be to you. This is particularly true when you're in a place like a restaurant, movie theater, or elevator where there's no place for people to escape to. So, mind the space you are in. A good rule of thumb is to allow a minimum of ten feet from the nearest person.

Get up and move if you have to. If you're in a crowded place where this is not an option, ask the person calling if you can call them back later.

Secondly, there is no need to speak loudly. Every cell phone has a built-in microphone that is more sensitive than the one on a wired phone. If you do yell into the receiver, the person on the other end of the line is probably holding the phone away from their ear (or turning the volume down) and thinking about how inconsiderate you are.

Similarly, watch the volume of your ringtone. There is no need to startle or annoy those around you when you receive a call. Determine what a reasonable level is, and be mindful of the selection you make to signal an incoming call. Putting your phone on vibrate is always a good option.

You also need to consider the company you are in. If you receive a call, and it is important, make sure that you properly excuse yourself. Do not make the person or people you are with think they are less important than the caller.

Finally, do not forget to turn your phone off before you go into a meeting or other important business function. Your focus needs to be on the people in the room, not on your phone.

E. Comprehension Check: *Without* looking back at the article, list (at least) five rules for using cell phones politely. What were the reasons for each one?

1. _____

2. _____

3. _____

4. _____

5. _____

F. Rethink: What other cell phone rules could you add to those listed in the article above? Draw on your own experience.

Section 4 ◆ Activity: Cell phone commercial

Directions: You work for a cell phone company. Your boss has just asked you to come up with some ideas for a funny commercial to promote a new phone with Internet access. You have fifteen minutes to make your pitch for a 30-second spot to the company president. Use the storyboard below to sequence the scenes. Be sure to use both words and pictures. To help you get started, think about cell phone commercials that you have seen and what made them effective or not.

1	2	3
4	5	6
7	8	9

◆ Showing Interest ◆ and Expressing Appreciation

Section 1 ◆ Starting Point: Treating people well

A. Warm Up: Discuss the following questions with a partner.

1. Do you have a good relationship with your family and friends? How about with your co-workers and the people you do business with?

2. Do you treat others the way you want to be treated? Explain your answer.

3. Do you think respect, politeness, and good manners can help build and maintain long-term business relationships? Why or why not?

B. Group Work:

First underline the words you are not sure of and clarify their meanings with your classmates. Then circle the five most important things to you. If there is something you value that is not on the list, write it in the margin.

Adaptability	Honesty	Respect
Being articulate	Humor	Responsibility
Commitment	Imagination	Self-discipline
Contribution	Integrity	Spontaneity
Creativity	Knowledge	Success
Decisiveness	Logic	Taking risks
Dignity	Optimism	Talent
Efficiency	Orderliness	Tolerance
Excellence	Peace	Truth
Friendship	Politeness	Wealth
Having courage	Quality	Wisdom
Helping others	Reliability	Working hard

Now answer the following questions.

1. Why are these five things important to you?
2. Why is it important to recognize and respect the values that other people hold?
3. How do differences in values lead to problems in communication and conflicts with other people at work?

C. As a Class: Answer the questions below.

1. What does it mean to "save face"?
2. Have you ever been in a position where you had to save face?
3. In a business context, what are the potential consequences of not saving face?

Section 2 ◆ Communication Strategies: Showing Interest

⊙ CD 1 track 7

Part 1: Read, listen to, and say these sentences and phrases.

Showing interest

What are you working on?
How's it coming along?
I think you did a nice/great job with/on ___.
What's going on with you?

Asking about thoughts and feelings

Are you OK?
What's on your mind?/Is something on your mind?
What are you thinking about?
You seem a little preoccupied with something.
Is there anything you want to talk about?
Is something bothering you?

Making sure something is fine

Is that OK/all right?
Are you sure/positive?

Being understanding

No problem. I understand.
Take your time. There's no rush.
That's not your fault.
I'd be happy to ___ if you like.

Expressing appreciation

Thanks for all your help.
Thanks for everything you've done.
Thanks a million. I owe you big time.
I really appreciate your help (with that).
You've been very helpful.
I couldn't have done it without you.

Responding to appreciation

You're welcome.
(It was) My pleasure.
Don't mention it.
Anytime.
If you need ___, just let me know.
No problem.
Not at all.

Part 2: Fill in the blanks with the phrases in **bold** type. When you're finished, read the dialogs with a partner. Then switch roles and read the dialogs again.

⊙ CD 1 track 8

I owe you big time   **appreciate**   **I thought you did a great job**
Don't mention it   **Thanks**   **What's going on**   **a million**
Seriously   **What are you working on**

A: _____ ?

B: Some visual aids. I have to give another presentation next week.

A: Really? _____ with the last one.

B: _____ . I really _____
that. _____ with you?

A: I'm finishing up the report we were working on.

B: Hey, thanks _____. _____ .

A: No problem.

B: _____! I don't think I could get this presentation
done without your help.

A: _____ .

Are you sure   **stressed out**   **I'd be happy to**
Is there something on your mind   **That's not your fault**

A: You seem a little _____. _____
_____?

B: I just got off the phone with a client who's really upset.

A: What happened?

B: Something with the delivery. The package was damaged when it arrived.

A: _____ .

B: I know, but he's blaming us.

A: _____ call the delivery company if you like.

B: Thanks, but I'll take care of it this afternoon.

A: _____ ?

B: Yeah. This is something I have to deal with.

I couldn't have done it without you   **Are you positive**   **Take your time**
just let me know   **rush**   **My pleasure**   **thank you for all your help**

A: When do you need me to check the sales figures?

B: _____ . There's no _____.

A: _____ ? Isn't there a deadline?

B: Usually there is, but not this time. Just check them when you can.

A: OK. Oh, I wanted to _____ at the orientation for new trainees. _____

_____.

B: _____ . If you need help again next month, _____ .

Part 3: With a partner, create and practice a dialog based on the following flow chart.

> Use business communication strategies from this chapter to help you. When you are finished, switch roles. Create and practice a similar dialog *without* using the flow chart.

A1: Show interest by asking what your partner is working on.

    B1: Say that you are working on a report. Ask your partner what's going on with him or her.

A2: Say that you are killing time before a meeting.

    B2: Use a rejoinder. Then ask if your partner is feeling okay (as you notice that she or he looks tired).

A3: Respond by saying you're fine. You're tired because you stayed up late finishing the contract for the meeting.

    B3: Thank your partner for his or her hard work (as you worked on most of this together).

A4: Respond to appreciation. Then tell your partner that she or he can leave early today.

    B4: Make sure this is fine.

A5: Say there's no rush with the report.

    B5: Express appreciation.

A6: Use a conversation closer (you have to go to the meeting).

    B6: Respond to the conversation. Tell your partner to have a great weekend.

A7: Respond to your partner.

Part 4: Use role play to act out the following situations. When you are finished, switch roles and practice again.

Situation 1

Your partner (who feels a lot of stress at work) doesn't look good. Ask if s/he is okay.

Situation 2

Express appreciation for something your partner has done to help you.

Part 5: Do you help build self-esteem in others by regularly showing interest and expressing appreciation? With a classmate, ask and answer the following questions to find out.

☞ When was the last time you paid someone a compliment?

☞ Do you make an effort to check in on people and see how they are doing (whether in person, over the phone, or via email)?

☞ Do you offer someone help when you see that they need it?

☞ Do you usually focus on the positive in others rather than finding fault or criticizing?

☞ Are you receptive to and open-minded about other people's thoughts, ideas, and opinions?

☞ Do you make sure to show gratitude for any help others have given you?

Section 3 ◆ Reading: When your boss is difficult to deal with

Having a bully for a boss can cause you a lot of anxiety at work. With the following exercises and article, you will have an opportunity to examine this issue and express your opinions about it.

A. Activate: What type of people have you had to work for in the past? Describe their personal qualities.

B. Discuss: Below are some descriptions of difficult people to work for. What are some effective strategies for dealing with each one? Write your ideas in the box.

Bullies: They know what your weak points are and how to exploit them. Teasing, sarcasm, and humiliation are their weapons of choice – all of which affect your performance on the job, your ability to concentrate, and your overall confidence.

```



```

Controllers: They want to micromanage every part of your job and control everything that goes on in the office.

```



```

Tyrants: There is one way do to things – their way or the highway. "Shape up or ship out" seems to be their motto.

```



```

Avoiders: They have a habit of putting things off until a deadline looms, because they are both unorganized and fearful about making the wrong decision. They are open to ideas but too paralyzed to act on them in a timely manner.

```



```

Blockheads: They don't know what they are doing – and everybody knows it. Decisions are often made that baffle employees. This comes from a lack of experience, a lack of knowledge, and/or inadequate information.

```



```

Can you think of any other types of difficult bosses and how to handle them?

C. Read: Read the following article.

Dealing with a difficult boss is never easy. Everyone has a story or two to tell. And more often than not, it is a feeling of being treated disrespectfully that affects us the most deeply. This cuts to the core of our ego and makes us feel a range of negative emotions on and away from the job.

Rather than letting your boss get you down, however, there are a few things you can do to improve your situation at work. First of all, because being a difficult person is part of their personality, it is highly unlikely that you will be able to affect how your boss acts. Instead, change the way you view and respond to their behavior. Try to understand the reasons why your boss is hard to deal with and devise tactics that will reduce your frustration and anger. One immediate thing you can do is adjust the way you view criticism. Instead of being baited and reacting defensively as if it is a personal attack, acknowledge what your boss is saying and see criticism as useful information to improve your performance on the job. If your boss criticizes your work, it clearly means that they have their own idea on how something should be done. So why not ask them for their advice on how your work can be improved? If you take this a step further and be proactive, you could prevent potential problems before they arise. Well-timed discussions with your boss in advance can minimize their negative actions later when things go wrong.

A second thing you can do is make sure that you are professional at all times. Be the model employee, someone they can always count on. You may not like your boss, but you are being paid to get the job done and carry out what they ask you to do in a dutiful manner. Exceed expectations and gain respect in return. You can also help yourself by reflecting on your own job performance. Regularly check to see where you can make improvements and act accordingly. This will show your boss how seriously you take your job and how devoted you are to doing the best you possibly can.

Finally, positively communicate any issue or concern you may have. This can lead to successful resolution of the matter. One way to do this is to arrange to meet with your boss several times in order to find out what they expect and need from you, and then discuss how you can meet those expectations and needs.

If for some reason making the changes above does not help, you may want to see if other people in your office feel the same way you do. The adage "power in numbers" holds true here. You could also keep a detailed written record of any unpleasant and difficult interactions. This could prove useful if you feel that your job is in danger or you need to explain what is going on to someone higher up on the management chain.

D. Comprehension Check: Are the following statements true (T) or false (F)? If a statement is false, rewrite it to make it true.

1. ____ The feeling of being treated disrespectfully by our boss affects us the most deeply.

2. ____ It is not difficult to change the way your boss acts toward you.

3. ____ Changing the way you view criticism can help reduce the amount of frustration and anger you feel.

4. ____ If your boss criticizes your work, it means that they do not have an idea about how something should be done.

5. ____ Discussions in advance of a problem could save you a lot of difficulties later.

6. ____ In order to be professional, you will have to learn to like your boss.

7. ____ By going beyond what you are asked to do, you will likely earn the respect of your boss.

8. ____ Regularly reflecting on your own job performance is a waste of time.

Using these statements as a guide (both the correct and corrected ones), try to summarize the article in your own words.

E. Rethink: The "Focus" section describes some difficult people to work *for*. It also gives each type a name. Can you think of some difficult people to work *with*? Draw on your own experiences in the workplace. Think of a name for each one. Can you apply the same strategies for dealing with a difficult boss to dealing with an unpleasant co-worker?

Section 4 ◆ Activity: Johari Window

Background: The Johari Window is a model that helps us understand relationships and interactions among people. It was developed by American psychologists Joseph Luft and Harry Ingham in the 1950s while researching group dynamics. It looks like this:

Arena	Blind
Hidden Area	Unknown Area

❧ The **arena** contains information you know about yourself and that others know about you (*e.g.* family, job, hobbies).

❧ The **hidden area** contains information you know about yourself but do not tell to other people (*e.g.* life experiences, hopes, dreams).

❧ The **blind area** represents what you do not know about yourself but what others know about you (*e.g.* attitudes, prejudices, weaknesses).

❧ The **unknown area** is the undiscovered part of you. It contains information about you that neither you nor others know (*e.g.* unremembered experiences or undiscovered talents).

Exercise: Copy the Johari Window on a blank piece of paper. Then choose six adjectives from the list below that describe your personality. On a separate sheet of paper, write them down. Keep your list hidden.

able	extroverted	mature	self-assertive
accepting	friendly	modest	self-conscious
adaptable	giving	nervous	sensible
bold	happy	observant	sentimental
brave	helpful	organized	shy
calm	idealistic	patient	silly
caring	independent	powerful	spontaneous
cheerful	ingenious	proud	sympathetic
clever	intelligent	quiet	tense
complex	introverted	reflective	trustworthy
confident	kind	relaxed	warm
dependable	knowledgeable	religious	wise
dignified	logical	responsive	witty
energetic	loving	searching	

Using the same list of adjectives, ask your classmates (as many as possible) to select six words that they think describe your personality. Have each person you ask anonymously write their list on a small piece of paper, fold it up, and give it to you.

When everyone is done, unfold all of the small pieces of paper. In the *arena pane*, write down the adjectives that are on your list and at least one of your classmates' lists. If an adjective appears on several lists, make a note of it (*e.g.*, "able IIII" - four times). In the *hidden area pane*, only write down adjectives you selected and no one else did. In the *blind area*, only write down adjectives your classmates selected and you didn't. All of the adjectives not selected by you or your classmates remain in the *unknown area pane*.

If you have more adjectives in the arena pane, this means that you practice self-disclosure (*i.e.*, you are comfortable sharing appropriate information about yourself in give-and-take relationships with other people) and are willing to accept and learn from feedback (positive or negative). If you have more adjectives in the blind pane, you should take a critical look at how other people see you and reflect on possible changes you can make to improve how you interact with others. If you have more adjectives in the hidden pane, you should consider opening yourself up to other people more than you do now. This will lead to better understanding, cooperation, and trust, while minimizing the potential for confusion, misunderstanding, and poor communication.

Reaction: Was the Johari Window revealing in any way? Did any of the adjectives selected by your classmates surprise you? Did the exercise make you think about how others perceive you? What did you learn about yourself?

◆ Maintaining Understanding ◆

Section 1 ◆ Starting Point: Active listening

A. Warm Up: Discuss the following questions with a partner.

1. Do you think you're a good listener? Is the person in the picture a good listener? Why do you think so?

2. When was the last time you found yourself in any of the following situations:

   ◉ During a conversation, you were thinking about how to respond rather than actually listening.

   ◉ You were daydreaming while someone was talking to you, which caused you to miss chunks of the conversation.

   ◉ Your lack of interest in the conversation caused you to tune the speaker out, although you pretended to continue listening.

   ◉ You started thinking about something you had to do later, or a (personal) problem that arose earlier, causing you to catch only bits and pieces of the conversation.

   ◉ You abruptly changed the topic of conversation to something that you were interested in.

   ◉ You constantly interrupted the person you were speaking to (or finished sentences for them).

3. What can ineffective listening (*i.e.,* misunderstanding, misinterpreting, or forgetting) lead to?

   How costly is ineffective listening in your personal life and at work? Consider the following fact:

   Communication involves message reception and interpretation. Studies of communication have routinely found that nearly everyone listens more than they talk, reads more than they write, and spends a lot more time receiving messages than sending them.

4. After listening to someone, can you accurately recall and restate what they said?

B. Pair Work:

Active listening is listening intently. This enables you to gain important information, be more effective in interpreting a message, gather data to make sound decisions, and respond appropriately to the messages you hear. To listen actively, think about how you would want to be listened to. In order to see how effective your active listening skills are, put a ✔ next to any of the following things you do in a typical conversation with someone. As you are working through the list, discuss what you do well and what you could do better.

- ☐ Put the speaker at ease by helping her or him feel free to talk. This includes being patient and allowing the speaker plenty of time to communicate their message.
- ☐ Be sincerely interested in what the other person is talking about by giving them your full attention and minimizing external and internal distractions (*i.e.* face the speaker, maintain eye contact, be attentive, and make the speaker feel important).
- ☐ Refrain from interrupting the speaker while they are communicating a message.
- ☐ Use rejoinders, give an occasional nod, and ask pertinent questions to show that you are interested and following along.
- ☐ "Mirror" the conversation (*i.e.,* ask questions and give feedback to the speaker to help them clarify their feelings, behavior and thinking).
- ☐ Put yourself in the other person's place so that you can see her or his point of view.
- ☐ Don't antagonize the speaker (*i.e.,* criticize ideas, argue, or express overly strong opinions).
- ☐ Watch for nonverbal messages by observing the speaker's body language, gestures, and physical distance from you for hidden messages.
- ☐ Focus on the main points by looking for the principal message of the words and filtering out anything that is nonessential.
- ☐ Sense how the speaker is feeling and determine what they are *not* saying.

Can you think of anything else you can do to be a better listener?

C. As a Class:

Nonverbal messages are an important part of active listening. They are used to create impressions, manage interaction, express emotions, send relational messages (*e.g.* power, respect, affection), convey or detect deception, and persuade. Below are some common examples. What can be interpreted by each one?

Example: standing with hands on hips – *readiness* or *aggression*

☞ sitting with legs crossed, foot kicking slightly
☞ arms crossed on chest
☞ pinching bridge of nose, eyes closed
☞ tapping or drumming fingers
☞ stroking chin
☞ looking down, face turned away
☞ pulling or tugging at ear
☞ raising eyebrow
☞ frowning
☞ hand over mouth
☞ clenching fists
☞ yawning

Can you think of other examples of nonverbal messages to convey:

☞ impatience
☞ frustration
☞ boredom
☞ doubt
☞ displeasure
☞ disbelief
☞ nervousness
☞ concern
☞ interest
☞ anger

Section 2 ♦ Communication Strategies: Maintaining understanding

⊙ CD 1 track 9

Part 1: Read, listen to, and say these sentences and phrases.

Asking for repetition

> Could you please repeat that?
> Could you please say that again?
> I didn't catch that. Could you say that one more time, please?
> I missed the first part. Would you mind repeating it?
> I'm sorry. What did you say?
> Would you run that by me again?
> You lost me. What was that again?

Repeating

> Sure/Of course. What I said was ____.
> Oh/Sorry. Let me repeat that. I said ____.

Asking for clarification

> Are you saying ____?
> What (exactly) do you mean by ____?
> So, you're saying we should ____?
> Could you explain what you mean by ____?
> What does ____ mean?/ Does that mean ____?
> What do you mean by that?
> Would you mind explaining that in a little more detail?

Clarifying

> What I'm trying to say is ____.
> What I mean (to say) is ____.
> What I meant was ____.
> Let me put it another way/this way.

Checking for understanding

> Are you following me?/Are you with me?
> Do you know what I mean?
> Do you know what I'm saying?
> Was that clear?/Is that clear enough?

Summarizing

> You said ____, right?
> What you're saying is ____?
> You think/believe that ____?
> Let me get this straight. You mean ____?

Part 2: Fill in the blanks with the phrases in **bold** type. When you're finished, read the dialogs with a partner. Then switch roles and read the dialogs again.

⊙ CD 1 track 10

didn't catch that   Would you mind explaining
What exactly do you mean by mission
Could you say that one more time, please

A: Today, I'm going to explain how to write a business plan. The first thing you have to do is define your mission. What do you want to achieve?

B: Excuse me. _____?

A: Mission means purpose and vision for your company. This sets the tone for all actions taken on a daily basis. The next thing you need to do is set your goals and objectives for the business.

B: I _____. _____?

A: Of course. What I said was you need to set goals and objectives.

B: _____ goals and objectives in a little more detail?

A: No problem. What do you want to achieve in the short term and long term? Think about things like how much money you hope to make and how many customers you want to have.

Would you run that by me   Is that clear enough
Could you please repeat that   Are you saying
What do you mean by that

A: The third thing you have to do is figure out your niche.

B: Niche? _____?

A: A niche is a particular specialty – what it is that you offer and provide that is different from other people in the market. _____?

B: Yes. Thanks. Go on.

A: OK. The fourth thing you need to do is know your market.

B: _____?

A: You must know your market. In other words, you need to have a broad picture of the market you're entering into. This will help you handle and maximize your potential business growth. Once you do that, then you need to learn about your customer.

B: _____ again?

A: Sure. I said that you have to learn about your customer. This is one of the most important aspects of running a business. Understanding and defining why they do what they do is the key to success.

B: _____ that this is the most important step?

A: Well, it is a very important step, but, no, that's not what I'm saying. All of the steps I'm telling you about are important.

Are you following   get this straight   I missed the first part   Was that clear

So far, so good   Would you mind repeating it

A: Now, on to the sixth step – research the demand for your business.

B: Excuse me. _____. You said something about demand. _____?

A: Research the demand. Then you have to set your marketing goals and define your marketing strategy. The goals relate to your product, your price, your distribution, and your promotions. You will also need to plan in detail how you will achieve these goals. _____ me?

B: _____.

A: Now, the last thing you need to do is put your plan into action. Move from preparation to actually doing business. And that's about it. _____
_____?

B: I think so, but let me _____. You said the first thing I have to do is . . .

Part 3: With a partner, create and practice a dialog based on the following flow chart. Use business communication strategies from this chapter to help you. When you're finished, switch roles. Create and practice a similar dialog **without** using the flow chart.

A1: Tell your partner that you are going to explain how to use a stockbroker. Begin by saying that you have to do some research.

B1: Ask for clarification.

A2: Clarify. Then say that step two is selecting a brokerage that meets your needs.

B2: You don't know what "brokerage" means. Ask for clarification.

A3: Clarify by saying it's a company that's engaged in buying and selling stocks and bonds for clients. Then move on to step three – read the brokerage agreement very carefully. And do not be afraid to ask questions.

B3: You missed the last part. Ask for repetition.

A4: Repeat (do not be afraid to ask questions). Then explain step four – open an account with the brokerage of your choice.

B4: Ask for clarification.

A5: Clarify. Then explain step five – research stocks and follow market news. Check for understanding.

B5: Say that you understand.

A6: Explain step six – call the broker and ask for a quote on the stock you want to buy or sell, and then decide what kind of order to place and place it.

B6: Ask for clarification.

A7: Clarify. Then explain step seven – get confirmation; make sure the broker complied with your order. Tell your partner that that is all there is to it.

B7: Use a rejoinder.

A8: Check for understanding.

B8: Summarize.

A9: Respond to your partner.

Part 4: Role-play the following situation. When you are finished, switch roles.
Repeat as necessary.

Person A

Talk about a complicated problem you had to deal with, a challenging project you
worked on, or a news story you read about or watched on television. Make sure it
is not easy to explain simply and that there are lots of details. Repeat and clarify
when needed, and check for understanding occasionally.

Person B

As your partner is talking, ask for repetition and clarify often. In fact, for
practice, do these things more often than you would need to normally. When
your partner is finished, summarize what they said.

Part 5:

In groups, describe experiences where you had a hard time maintaining
understanding with someone. Think about language barriers, context
(where the conversation was taking place), and situation (what was happening
at the time).

Section 3 ◆ Reading: Effective communication

Whether you are speaking to someone in person, talking on the phone, or sending an email or fax, you need to be able to communicate effectively. With the following exercises and article, you will have an opportunity to examine this issue and express your opinions about it.

A. Activate: Which of the following communication barriers do you face at work? Check each box that applies.

☐ *Physical* (environmental problems – office layout, equipment/technology, background noise, temperature)

☐ *Structural* (system-level problems – lack of supervision or training, uncertainty about roles and responsibilities)

☐ *Situational* (problems with task – lack of information or knowledge, not understanding fully, short of time, not thinking it through, failure to explore alternatives)

☐ *Attitudinal* (problems with colleagues – personality conflicts, poor management, work dissatisfaction, bad mood)

☐ *Psychological* (state of mind stemming from issues in personal life, both positive and negative)

☐ *Physiological* (personal discomfort as a result of ill health – cold, hangover, injury)

☐ *Linguistic* (trouble grasping difficult words or concepts, inability to comprehend poor explanations, confusion resulting from misunderstood message)

☐ *Personal* (individual filters – generalizing, stereotyping, prejudice, preconceptions, fixed ideas, selective hearing, assumptions, jumping to conclusions)

B. Discuss: If the difficulties posed by these communication barriers are not recognized and dealt with effectively, what are some potential outcomes? Add to the list below.

> Misunderstandings
> Frustration and tension
> Loss of business

Now give some specific examples of the communication barriers you face at work these days. Explain why they are problematic for you and your company. Then discuss ways to effectively deal with each one.

C. Focus: Draw lines to match each part of the communication process on the left with its definition on the right.

Parts of the communication process   **Definitions**

Parts of the communication process	Definitions
1. Sender	Verbal and nonverbal reactions to what is spoken
2. Message	Who is being spoken to
3. Channel	What is spoken and how it is spoken
4. Receiver	Surrounding environment or broader culture
5. Feedback	Who is speaking
6. Context	In person, over the phone, via email or fax

Now put the six parts of the communication process in the six boxes below. (HINT: Follow the order of the parts above!)

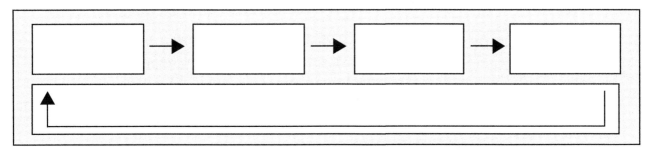

D. Read: Read the following article.

Dale Carnegie was an American writer, lecturer, and pioneer in self-improvement. He became famous for courses he developed that emphasized public speaking, interpersonal skills, salesmanship, and corporate training. His most notable self-help book, *How to Win Friends and Influence People*, won him a national following. It has sold over 10 million copies since it was first published in 1936. The book appeals to people who want to change their life, and gives tips and strategies for communicating with others. At its core, the book emphasizes that pleasing other people is a duty and a route to success in personal and professional relationships. Carnegie provided seven guidelines toward these ends which are as valid today as they were then:

- ☞ Never criticize, condemn, or complain
- ☞ Show interest in others
- ☞ Smile
- ☞ Use people's names
- ☞ Listen carefully
- ☞ Talk about topics of interest to the other person
- ☞ Make the person feel important

The book's principal message is, "Do unto others as you would have them do unto you."

DALE CARNEGIE
presented by
THE CITY SALESMAN'S CLUB
MUNICIPAL AUDITORIUM — BIRMINGHAM, ALABAMA
FRIDAY, MAY 27, 1928 — 8:15 P. M.

Unlike many other books of its kind, *How to Win Friends and Influence People* is not based on dry theory alone. Instead, it is rooted in the experiences of students in courses Dale Carnegie taught who have applied the ideas to find out what really works in everyday interactions.

E. Comprehension Check: Can you remember what you read? Answer the following questions **without** looking back at the article.

1. Who was Dale Carnegie?
2. What did he become famous for?
3. What was the name of his most notable self-help book?
4. How many copies of the book have been sold?
5. When was it published?
6. Who does the book appeal to?
7. What kinds of tips and strategies does the book give?
8. What does the book emphasize at its core?
9. What seven guidelines did Carnegie provide in his book?
10. What is the book's principal message?

Read the article again and check your answers.

Have you read or would you be interested in reading *How to Win Friends and Influence People*? Do you agree with the book's principal message? Why or why not?

F. Rethink: How can we remove barriers and improve our communication skills at work? What are some specific things we can do for each part of the communication process?

Section 4 ◆ Activity: Gender differences in communication

Men and women often have different communication styles. Awareness of these differences – both at work and away from it – is important. It can help you reduce communication barriers.

Directions: Read the statement in *italics*. Decide if it is truer for men or for women or if it is not a gender issue. Write "Men," "Women," or "Both" on each line.

Purpose of a conversation

_____ *Maintain independence and display knowledge and skill*

_____ *Build rapport and connections with people*

Problems (that arise at work)

_____ *Seek empathy and understanding; want to be listened to carefully*

_____ *See these as challenges they must deal with by themselves*

Colleagues

_____ *More likely to criticize than compliment their colleagues*

_____ *More likely to compliment than criticize their colleagues*

Deadlines

_____ *Are more direct and forceful*

_____ *Tend to use phrases to express apologies or gratitude when asking to get something done*

Recognition (for a job well done)

_____ *Spread good fortune and opportunities*

_____ *Boast and call attention to their achievement*

Meetings

_____ *Are more assertive and speak more often and longer*

_____ *Are less assertive and limit speaking time*

Now answer these questions with a partner or in a group, and discuss your differences.

1. Was it difficult for you to make a decision for each set of statements?

2. How accurate are these statements about men and women in the workplace?

3. Do you think that they are stereotypical in any way?

4. Do you think there is a (Western) cultural bias inherent in any of them?

5. Do you want to alter or add to any of the statements to make them more accurate for the place where you work?

6. How much does context affect differences in communication styles between men and women in the workplace?

7. Do you agree that it is important to have an awareness of differences in communication style? Why or why not?

◆ Questioning ◆

Section 1 ◆ Starting Point: Questions

A. Warm Up: Interview a classmate. When you are finished, switch roles.
For the time being, don't pay any attention to the line after each question.

1. What do you do? _____

2. Do you like your job? _____

3. What do you like most about your company or organization? _____

4. What are some common problems you run into at work? _____

5. You like your boss, don't you? _____

6. You'd like to work fewer hours, wouldn't you? _____

7. If you were the president of your company, what would you do differently?

   _____

8. If you had more vacation time, what would you like to do? _____

9. Can you tell me what you like or don't like about one of your co-workers?

   _____

10. What kind of bad decisions has your boss made since you started working here?

    _____

B. Group Work:

Work with your partner and make questions with the prompts below. Then put your questions to another pair. Again, for the time being, do not pay any attention to the lines after the questions.

1. Did you ___ last weekend? _____

2. How do you feel about ____? _____

3. Could you tell me why ____? (Could you elaborate more?) _____

4. You don't enjoy ____, right? _____

5. If you could change ____? _____

6. You want to ____, don't you? _____

7. Have you ____? _____

8. What sort of ____ do you like? _____

9. If you were in a position to make a difference in the world, ____?

    _____

10. What are the pros and cons of ____? (Can you explain that further?)

    _____

C. As a Class:

Ask your teacher some of the questions you posed to the other pair. See how she or he responds.

Section 2 ♦ Communication Strategies: Question types

⊙ CD 1 track 11

Part 1: Read, listen to, and say these sentences and phrases.

Closed (Yes/No) questions (*give facts, easy and quick to answer, help you remain in control of the conversation*)

Do/Did you ____?   Would you like ____?
Are/Have you ____?   Will you ____?

Open (Information) questions (*ask someone to think and reflect, give you opinions and feelings, hand control of conversation to the respondent*)

Why ____?/Where ____?   How do you think ____?
What do you like about ____?   What kind/sort of ____?
What do you think about ____?   What about ____?
How do you feel about ____?   What time ____?

Leading questions (*deliberately designed to make respondent think and reply in a certain way*)

Don't you ____?   ____, wouldn't you?
Is that right, ____?   ____, couldn't we?
I really like/dislike ____. What do you think ____?

Hypothetical questions (*get respondents to think about possibilities*)

If (you could) ____?
What if ____?
What's the worst/best ____?
What are the possible/potential ____?

Probing questions (*get more details or further information from respondent*)

Could you be more specific?
Could you give me an example?
Could you explain that further?
Could you elaborate more?
Could you tell me more about ____?
Why did you say ____?

Part 2: Go back to "Starting Point" and label each question in the first two sections. Write one of the five question types on the line.

Part 3: Fill in the blanks with the phrases in **bold** type. When you're finished, read the dialogs with a partner. Then switch roles and read the dialogs again.

⊙ CD 1 track 12

Don't you   What do you think about   Have you
What do you mean

A: _____ seen our new website?
B: Yeah, I just checked it out this morning.
A: _____ it?
B: It's better than what we had before.
A: _____?
B: The layout, graphics, and colors are much nicer. And it's easier to navigate.
_____ agree?

couldn't we   What's the worst   What if   Do you

A: _____ have to go in to work this weekend?

B: Yep.

A: Me, too. I'm not very happy about it.

B: I'm not either, but our deadline is right around the corner.

A: _____ we stayed later during the week instead?
We could get everything done by Friday, _____?
_____ case scenario if we didn't?

B: Well, for starters, we'd lose the contract.

Could you explain that   I know what you're saying
How do you think   what do you think will happen   elaborate

A: _____ we're doing with our public relations
campaign?

B: Not bad, but we need to work on our press conferences. They need to
be done within a cross-cultural framework.

A: I'm not sure I follow you. _____ further?

B: Speaking styles and the content used differ across cultures. What works
here in this country might not translate well abroad.

A: I think I understand, but could you _____ more?

B: In this country, the messages we send are more direct, straightforward. But
it's different in a place like, say, Japan or Korea.

A: _____ , but that might be hard to
do under the circumstances. If we don't make any changes, _____
_____?

B: I think we'll be asking for trouble.

Part 4: With a partner, create and practice a dialog based on the following flow chart. Use business communication strategies from this chapter to help you. When you are finished, switch roles. Create and practice a similar dialog **without** using the flow chart.

A1: Ask if your partner likes his/her new computer.

        B1: Say that you do.

A2: Ask how much it cost.

        B2: Say that your company bought it for you.

A3: Use a rejoinder. Then ask if your partner would get the same computer if s/he had to pay for it.

        B3: Say that you would.

A4: Ask an open question (Why).

        B4: Say that it has all the features that you want.

A5: Ask a probing question.

        B5: Talk about the design, processor (fast), and memory (a lot).

A6: Ask an open question about the hard drive.

        B6: Say that it's much more than you need.

A7: Ask a hypothetical question about Macs versus PCs (switching).

        B7: Say that you wouldn't switch.

A8: Ask an open question (Why).

        B8: Say that you're satisfied with what you have now.

Part 5: Choose one of the following topics. Ask your partner some questions about it. Make sure to use different types. When you are finished, switch roles. Repeat as necessary.

    ☞ A famous company, product, or service

    ☞ A renowned business leader

    ☞ A current story or issue in the news

    ☞ A problem at work

    ☞ Plans for the future

    ☞ City or country you live in

Section 3 ♦ Reading: Bloom's taxonomy

Benjamin Bloom was a University of Chicago psychologist who made important contributions to the classification of educational objectives. Although the taxonomy (classification system) he proposed in 1956 was aimed at educators with the intent of creating a holistic education for students, his work is relevant for a wide range of academic disciplines, including business. With the following exercises and article, you will have an opportunity to examine his ideas and express your opinions about them.

A. Activate: Discuss the following questions with a partner.

1. What have you learned in the first five units of this book? How much information can you recall?

2. What do you think is the main point of this book? What is the author trying to help you do?

3. How can you apply what you are learning in this book to your job?

4. What local, national, or international story in the news concerns you the most these days? What are some possible consequences, outcomes, or results of that situation?

5. In the 2006 film, "An Inconvenient Truth," U.S. statesman Al Gore urges humankind to confront global warming now or face devastating consequences in the future. Can you come up with any ideas to deal with this problem?

6. Think of a difficult problem your country faced in the past. What would you have done if you had wanted to do something about it?

B. Focus: "Thinking outside the box" means thinking beyond the usual way of doing things. How important is this in the business world? Can you give examples of business leaders or companies that clearly think outside the box? Are you a creative thinker, who comes up with unusual yet intelligent ideas and effective solutions?

C. Read: Read the following article.

In an effort to develop a classification of educational objectives, a group of educational psychologists led by Benjamin Bloom established human thinking skills into the following six categories:

☞ *Knowledge:* remembering or recalling learned information to draw out factual answers

☞ *Comprehension:* grasping the meaning of informational materials

☞ *Application:* applying previously learned information or knowledge to new and unfamiliar situations

☞ *Analysis:* breaking down information into parts or examining information

☞ *Synthesis:* applying prior knowledge and skills to combine elements into a pattern not there before

☞ *Evaluation:* judging or deciding according to some set of criteria, without real right or wrong answers

These categories represent levels of thought that increase in complexity (*i.e.* from simple recall to making serious judgments and decisions).

Asking people to think at higher levels, beyond simple recall, is an excellent way to stimulate their thought processes. Ostensibly, different types of questions require us to use different kinds or levels of thinking. Use the question prompts in the table below to get people at work to think more deeply and outside the box.

Knowledge	Comprehension
Who _____? When _____? Where _____? How many _____?	What was the main point of _____? What do you specifically remember _____? Can you state in your own words _____? What is the purpose of _____?
Application	**Analysis**
Can you think of another instance where _____? Can you relate _____ to your own experience? Could this have happened in/at _____? Would things be different if _____?	What are some possible outcomes? How is this similar to (or different from) _____? Why did/didn't _____ happen? What are some of the problems of _____?
Synthesis	**Evaluation**
How many ways can you _____? Can you develop a plan/proposal that would ___? If you had unlimited access, how would you ___? Can you come up with new ideas/uses for _____?	Do you think _____ is positive or negative? Is there a better solution to _____? How would you have handled _____? What changes would you make _____ (to)?

D. Comprehension Check: Write the thinking skill category next to its meaning **without** looking back at the article.

1. _____ applying prior knowledge and skills to combine elements into a pattern not there before

2. _____ grasping the meaning of informational materials

3. _____ judging or deciding according to some set of criteria, without real right or wrong answers

4. _____ remembering or recalling learned information to draw out factual answers

5. _____ applying previously learned information or knowledge to new and unfamiliar situations

6. _____ breaking down information into parts or examining information

Now answer the following questions.

1. Can you recall question prompts for each thinking skill category?

2. Why is it important to ask different types of questions?

3. How can Bloom's questions get you to think more deeply about the work you do?

E. Rethink:

What similarities do you notice between the question types shown earlier in this unit and the thinking skill category questions devised by Bloom?

Section 4 ♦ Activity: 20 Questions

Directions: Pretend that you have the opportunity to interview the Chief Executive
Officer (CEO) of a world-famous company (*e.g.,* Steve Jobs or Bill Gates) or some
other well-known public figure (*e.g.,* a politician or entertainer). You have been asked
to prepare 20 questions based on the types you learned about in this chapter.

With a partner, decide who you want to interview. Write your questions together.
Then exchange them with those of with another pair. Hold mock interviews, with
one person being the interviewer and one person being the interviewee. The point
of this is to practice using a skill (asking questions). Therefore, answer all the
questions – even if you don't know what the answer is. If necessary, either say,
"I'd rather not answer that" or "Let's move on to the next question," or simply
make up an answer. Repeat as necessary so that each of the four people has an
opportunity to participate.

♦ Offering and Asking for Assistance ♦

Section 1 ♦ Starting Point: Teamwork

A. Warm Up: How are the following inspirational quotes from the world of sports applicable in the workplace? Discuss with a partner.

> The strength of the team is each individual member. The strength of each member is the team.
> – *Phil Jackson, N.B.A. Coach, Los Angeles Lakers and Chicago Bulls*

> Individual commitment to a group effort – that is what makes a team work, a company work, a society work, a civilization work.
> – *Vince Lombardi, N.F.L. Coach, Green Bay Packers and Washington Redskins*

B. Group Work: Discuss the following questions.

1. What is teamwork?
2. How important is teamwork where you work?
3. What was the last team project you worked on? Was your team able to complete the project successfully? Why or why not?

C. As a Class: Identify some companies that clearly have strong global business teams. Discuss the reasons for their success.

⊙ CD 1 track 13

Section 2 ♦ Communication Strategies:
Offering and asking for assistance

Part 1: Read, listen to, and say these sentences and phrases.

Offering assistance

Need some help?/Need a hand? [1-3, 9-10]*
Can I give you a hand? [1-3, 9-10]
Would you like some help? [1-3, 9-10]
Do you need any help? [1-3, 9-10]
Is there anything you need help with? [5, 10]
Is there anything I can do (for you)? [5, 10]
(Here,) Let me help you with that. [4, 6, 10]
I'll take care of it. [4, 6, 10]
If you need any help, all you have to do is ask. [7]
If you need help with anything, please let me know. [7-8]
If there's anything I can do to help, please let me know. [7-8]
Let me know if there's anything I can do. [7-8]

*See corresponding numbers below for an appropriate response.

Responding to offers of assistance

1. Oh, that'd be great.
2. Do you mind?
3. If you don't mind.
4. Are you sure?
5. As a matter of fact,/Actually, there is.
6. Really? Thanks!
7. OK. Thanks!
8. I will. Thanks!
9. No. I got it. (Thanks.)
10. I'm OK. (Thanks./Thanks for asking.)

Asking for assistance

Can you help me with this?
Can you give me a hand?
Can you take care of this for me?
Would you mind ___ for me?
Could you ___ for me?
Would you mind helping me for a minute?

Requesting a favor

Could you do me a favor?   Would you mind doing me a favor?
Can I ask you a favor?   If you don't mind, I have a favor to ask.

Part 2: Fill in the blanks with the phrases in **bold** type. When you are finished, read the dialogs with a partner. Then switch roles and read the dialogs again.

⊙ CD 1 track 14

I got it   Do you mind   Could you do me a favor
Would you like some help   need any help   Can you

A: You've got quite a stack there. Do you _____ putting those files away?

B: _____? That'd be great.

A: _____? Tell the receptionist that I'm running a little late.

B: No problem. Do you want me to call her right now?

♦   ♦   ♦

A: Those boxes look really heavy. _____?

B: No. _____. Thanks.

♦   ♦   ♦

A: _____ take a look at this document and tell me if there are any mistakes? I've read it over too many times this morning.

B: Sure thing. Let's have a look.

Is there anything I can help you with   Are you sure   I will
so far   I'll take care of that   Can you take care of it
If you need help with anything

A: You should go home and rest. _____.

B: _____? There's still a lot that needs to be done.

♦   ♦   ♦

A: I know you have a lot to do today. _____, please let me know.

B: _____. Thanks!

♦   ♦   ♦

A: I haven't sent the fax yet. _____ for me?

B: Sure. What's the fax number?

♦   ♦   ♦

A: Your first day on the job can be pretty tough. _____ _____?

B: I'm OK _____. Thanks for asking.

Part 3: With a partner, create and practice a dialog based on the following flow chart. Use business communication strategies from this chapter to help you. When you are finished, switch roles. Create and practice a similar dialog **without** using the flow chart.

A1: Use a conversation starter.

B1: Say that you are stressed out.

A2: Ask why and inquire about what your partner is working on.

B2: Say that you are doing some data entry work that needs to be completed by lunch time.

A3: Ask why that is so stressful.

B3: Say that the data entry work is burdensome because you should be preparing for an important meeting later this afternoon.

A4: Offer some assistance.

B4: Respond affirmatively to offer of assistance.

A5: Say it is no problem as you have a lot of free time today.

B5: Express appreciation.

A6: Offer to help your partner prepare for the meeting, too.

B6: Respond to offer of assistance – say that you have to work on that by yourself.

A7: Use a rejoinder ("I see") and then ask about how to do the data entry work.

B7: Say, "Here, let me show you . . ."

Part 4: Practice offering assistance, asking for assistance, and requesting favors. Use as many different expressions as you can. When you are finished, switch roles and repeat.

Partner A	*Partner B*
1. Help put some supplies away. (Offer)	
	2. Help plan an office party. (Offer)
3. Fix the photocopier that is jammed. (Favor)	
	4. Send a package at the post office. (Ask)
5. Help proofread a report. (Offer)	
	6. Help make visual aids for a presentation. (Offer)
7. Pick someone up at the airport. (Ask)	
	8. Show new employee around the office. (Favor)
9. Help set up equipment for a workshop. (Offer)	
	10. Help move some office furniture. (Offer)
11. Confirm a restaurant reservation. (Ask)	
	12. Order some new toner for the printer. (Ask)
13. Help brainstorm new ideas for a project. (Offer)	
	14. Help organize documents for a meeting. (Offer)
15. Lead a meeting. (Favor)	
	16. Write a proposal. (Favor)
17. Help translate an email into English. (Offer)	
	18. Help do some Internet research. (Offer)
19. Format a document on the computer. (Ask)	
	20. Interview applicant for a job at company. (Ask)

Part 5: Have you ever worked with someone who relied on you too much? What is the best way to deal with someone who is requesting too many favors or asking for too much assistance?

Section 3 ◆ Reading: Being a team player

Being a team player is an essential part of most people's job. With the following exercises and article, you will have an opportunity to examine this issue and express your opinions about it.

A. Activate: Are you a good team player? Write one of the following numbers on the line next to each of the statements below.

5 = 100% true, 4 = mostly true, 3 = sometimes true, sometimes not, 2 = mostly untrue, 1 = 100% false

1. ____ I would rather work with a group than by myself.

2. ____ I find it easy to believe in and trust other people.

3. ____ I realize that sometimes I have the right answer and sometimes I do not.

4. ____ I am usually more cooperative than competitive.

5. ____ I enjoy working with a diverse group of people.

6. ____ I like the give-and-take that happens in a group.

7. ____ I believe that other people work as hard as I do.

8. ____ I have no problem sharing information, ideas, and recognition
with other people.

9. ____ I am flexible and easily adapt to changing circumstances.

10. ____ I exhibit interest and enthusiasm most of the time.

Add the numbers for all ten statements above. If you scored 40-50, you definitely have what it takes to be a good team player. If you scored 39 or less, take a closer look at these statements and see what you can do to improve your teamwork skills.

B. Discuss: With a partner, discuss the following question.

Do you think you are a good team player? Do you agree with your score?

C. Focus: Match each key characteristic of effective teams on the left with its explanation on the right. Use a process of elimination to help you (*i.e.*, match the ones you know first).

1. ___ *Purpose*   A. Made together as a group (whether consensus or majority)

2. ___ *Work environment*   B. Relaxed, comfortable atmosphere (feelings of belief and trust)

3. ___ *Team*   C. Shared control of team (not led by one person)

4. ___ *Assignments*   D. Constructive assessment of performance

5. ___ *Participation*   E. Roles are unambiguously defined (expectations are clear)

6. ___ *Open communication*   F. Clear and explicit goals and objectives for project or task

7. ___ *Contributions*   G. Broad spectrum of people, each with unique strengths

8. ___ *Leadership*   H. Individual performance is affirmed and honored

9. ___ *Decisions*   I. Active – each person takes initiative and fulfills responsibilities

10. ___ *Feedback*   J. Free expression of thoughts and ideas (no limitations)

D. Read: Read the following article.

To excel in today's business world, companies and organizations depend on teams to develop new products, achieve cost reductions, improve quality, increase productivity, and solve problems.

As a team is only as strong as the collective performance of those involved, each individual member must be committed, think collaboratively, and display competence. Being committed means taking initiative, working hard, doing your part, and helping make things happen. Collaboration involves a willingness to share information, knowledge, and experience, and to work cooperatively together to solve problems and reach a common goal. Competency is demonstrated through speaking up and expressing thoughts and ideas clearly, directly, and honestly.

Being part of a team also necessitates patience and understanding. This requires maintaining a positive attitude in the face of stressful situations and hardship, being tolerant of challenging personality traits and shifting moods, and showing respect and support for others.

Another important part of being a team player is seeing things from different points of view. Instead of always looking at something from a limited perspective, namely their own, team players need to imagine how the other people they are working with might view the same thing. This should result in an increased level of sensitivity to their colleagues.

Finally, team players need to be flexible and know how to adapt to situations that are constantly evolving. Team players must be prepared for the unexpected and embrace change, knowing that they can confidently handle both.

E. Comprehension Check: Fill in the blanks **without** looking back at the article.

1. A team player must be **c**_____, think **c**_____, and exude **c**_____.

2. Being part of a team necessitates **p**_____ and **u**_____.

3. Another important part of being a team is seeing things from a **d**_____ **p**_____ of **v**_____.

4. Team players also need to be **f**_____ and know how to **a**_____ to changing situations.

F. Rethink (Group Work): Read the text below.

Dr. Meredith Belbin is a world-renowned expert and advisor on organization and teams. He is best known for his team-role theory, which was developed through behavioral studies of managers from all over the world. Through his research, Belbin proposed nine roles – based on clusters of characteristics – that successful teams should have.

Coordinator: Has a clear idea of objectives and how to achieve them.

Shaper: Helps make things happen and get things going.

Plant: Thinks outside the box – offers new ideas and innovative ways for doing things.

Resource Investigator: Has many contacts and knows how to gather information.

Implementer: Is organized and effective at turning ideas into manageable tasks that can be achieved.

Team Worker: Is most aware, sensitive, and supportive of team members' needs and concerns.

Completer: Makes sure work is done by the deadline.

Monitor Evaluator: Considers all options and looks at things from different perspectives.

Specialist: Provides unique skills and knowledge.

Now answer the following questions:

1. Which role(s) do you typically take on when you work in a group? Why?

2. Do you think all of these roles are necessary for a work group to function successfully? Why or why not?

3. If you could be part of a work group with just four roles, which combination do you think would be most effective? Why?

Section 4 ◆ Activity: Who will survive?

Part 1: A group of nine people have just survived a plane crash in the middle of the South Pacific. The damage to the aircraft is severe and it is sinking quickly. Nothing except for a life raft can be saved – a raft that is only big enough for four people. With the aid and protection of the raft, it's possible to survive the crash and reach some land seen in the distance. Without the raft, the shark-infested waters will ensure certain death.

Who survives? Who doesn't? Work as a group and make a decision.

Here is a list of the survivors:

Jose – Pilot of the plane. He has a wife, three daughters, and six grandchildren. When he isn't flying, he is a volunteer in his community. He works for a youth outreach program.

Dahlia – Doctor. She is a medical doctor who has worked all over the world. She has treated patients with an incredible range of injuries and illnesses. Currently, she is the chief surgeon at a large hospital.

Boris – Chef. He is a celebrity cook who is famous for being able to take any combination of ingredients and turn them into a delicious meal. He has a charming personality and is instantly likeable.

Liu – Psychologist. She specializes in helping people recover from traumatic experiences. She has been on the frontlines of many disaster relief efforts all over Asia and Africa.

Izzy – Elementary school student. He is ten years old. His main interests are surfing and scuba diving. He is definitely no stranger to the water. He was on his way back home to his parents and two brothers.

Erika – Gardener. She has experience owning and operating many fruit and vegetable gardens. Her nickname is "Green Thumb" because she has an extraordinary ability to make plants grow well.

Min – Artist. He suffered a spinal cord injury in a car accident and is now a quadriplegic. Being confined to a wheelchair hasn't stopped him from producing great works of art and writing fascinating stories.

Adanna – Architect. She has won numerous awards for innovation in design. In addition to being full of brilliant ideas, she is very handy with tools. She currently lives in a solar-powered house she built by herself.

Mike – Biology teacher. He is a well-known scholar who has published his research in many academic journals. The focus of his work is tropical flora and fauna. He has spent a lot of time in tropical areas.

When you are finished, share your decision-making process with the class. Which four people did you choose? Why?

Part 2: The purpose of this activity is to discover how you work together as a group. In order to assess how well you did this, answer the following questions:

1. How did you reach your decision? Did you help each other come up with the best solution?

2. Did you work well together as a group?

3. Did everyone in your group participate actively?

4. Did everyone listen carefully to what each person had to say?

5. Did you ask a lot of questions to explore the issue in depth?

6. Did anyone try to dominate the discussion?

7. Did anyone feel that their contribution was not taken seriously or valued?

8. Did everyone feel free to express their thoughts and ideas?

9. What did you learn about your group? What was easy to do? What was challenging?

10. What would you try to do better next time?

◆ Stating Goals and Objectives ◆

Section 1 ◆ Starting Point: Goals and objectives

A. Warm Up: Discuss the following questions with a partner.

Part 1

1. Think about your past. Have you ever successfully reached a personal goal you set for yourself? What steps did you take to reach it?

2. What are some of your current professional goals? How do you plan to achieve them?

3. What are the goals of your company?

Part 2

1. Why is it sometimes difficult to reach goals you set for yourself?

2. What have been some of the biggest obstacles in your life that have made it difficult for you to achieve certain goals?

3. How has not reaching certain personal goals affected your life today?

B. Group Work: What is a "high achiever?" Are you a high achiever? Put a ✔ next to each characteristic that applies. Give examples from work (or school) for each box you checked.

Are you . . .?

☐ Highly curious

☐ A creative thinker

☐ Keenly observant

☐ Resourceful and enterprising

☐ Passionate about your work

☐ Dedicated, disciplined, and perseverant

☐ Self-confident

☐ Calm under pressure

☐ Able to think abstractly

☐ Effective at solving problems

☐ One who handles challenges effectively

☐ Fiercely competitive

☐ A risk taker

☐ One who learns from mistakes

☐ An opportunity creator (and seizer)

☐ Able to see the big picture and the details

C. As a Class:

Who are some of the highest achievers you know? How are they able to accomplish their goals so successfully?

Section 2 ♦ Communication Strategies: Stating goals and objectives

⊙ CD 1 track 15

Part 1: Read, listen to, and say these sentences and phrases.

Stating goals and objectives

Our objective/goal/aim (today) is (to) ___.

Our principal aim is to ___.

We're here today to ___.

Our agenda (today) is ___.

There are three things we have to do/discuss/talk about (today).

We have to (decide) ___ (by ___).

We need to figure out a way to ___ (by ___).

We need to come up with ___ (by ___).

We'll need to get everything done by ___.

If possible, we'd like to ___ by ___.

What we want to accomplish/do today is ___.

Let's (do) ___ first. Then we can focus on/take care of ___.

Our first priority is _____.

This is urgent. We must take care of it immediately.

Stating shared aims

Our goals/objectives are the same as yours.

Together we have to ___.

We're in agreement that ___.

We agree that ___.

It's important that we agree/see eye to eye on ___.

We're on the same page.

We've got the same objective(s)/goal(s).

Your ideas are right in line with ours/mine.

Part 2: Fill in the blanks with the phrases in **bold** type. When you are finished, read the dialogs with a partner. Then switch roles and read the dialogs again.

⊙ CD 1 track 16

take care of it immediately   figure out
We need to get everything done by   urgent   Our objective today is

A: We're going to launch two new products next year. _____
to identify price points for each one.

B: How are we going to do that?

A: Well, we have to _____ which price will maximize
income from the beginning.

B: How much time do we have to work on this?

A: _____ the end of the week.

B: The end of the week? That's not very much time.

A: I know, but this is _____. We have to _____
_____. So, before we do anything else, let's look at our
competitor's products and see what they're selling them for.

see eye to eye   right in line with ours   focus
We're here today to   priority   we agree that

A: _____ discuss the terms of the contract.

B: As far as we can tell, your ideas are _____.

A: So _____ construction on the new building will
begin at the end of the month?

B: Yes.

A: Good. It's important that we _____ on that.

B: Our first _____, then, is to check these documents. After
that, we can _____ on the budget and schedule for this project.

we'll have to get everything else done   our principal aim
If possible, I'd like to   We're in agreement   come up with

A: I think _____ at the workshop should be to tell
people how to invest their money successfully.

B: _____ there, but we don't have a lot of time to prepare.

A: I know. We'll need to _____ a rough outline before lunch.
And _____, including
visual aids, by Wednesday night.

B: _____ finish by Tuesday night. That'll
give us some time to practice the delivery.

A: Which is crucial. Good point. OK, the first thing we need to do is . . .

Part 3: With a partner, create and practice a dialog based on the following flow chart. Use business communication strategies from this chapter to help you. When you are finished, switch roles. Create and practice a similar dialog **without** using the flow chart.

Dialog – *Choose a famous company that sells products.*

A1: State goal and objectives – increase the company's bottom line.

B1: Ask how the company plans to do this.

A2: Say that it can start by gaining more market share – aim to increase profits by 10% next quarter.

B2: Suggest that this might be hard to achieve.

A3: Agree, but say it's possible if you strive to make customers more satisfied.

B3: Suggest a way to do this.

A4: State that customer satisfaction is one objective, then say that another one is to reduce manufacturing costs.

B4: Agree with your partner.

A5: Continue by saying that the company needs to increase the speed of processing orders.

B5: Note complaints made by customers about this recently.

A6: Say that these are the company's priorities, but other ideas are in the works.

B6: Respond to your partner.

Part 4: You work for a famous automobile company that is underperforming*. Being in the world's biggest and most competitive market, there are many situations you will have to deal with. Pretend you are in a meeting with colleagues from different divisions of your company and try to come up with possible solutions for the problems below. State your goals and objectives by answering the following questions: What do you want to achieve? What steps do you need to take in order to do this?

Think of an automobile company somewhere in the world that is not doing well. This will give you a context and focus for this activity.

Problems

1. Increased competition
2. Declining market share
3. New competitors entering your markets
4. Lack of new product development
5. Low product quality
6. Government regulation
7. A precarious financial position
8. Unclear vision of the future

Part 5: Share your solutions to the problems above with the class.

Section 3 ♦ Reading: Strategic planning

Strategic planning is a management tool that helps an organization improve its overall performance. With the following exercises and article, you will have an opportunity to examine this issue and express your opinions about it.

A. Activate: Work with a partner. To successfully achieve a business goal, you need to follow these four steps. Put them in order from "1" (first) to "4" (last).

___ Complete each scheduled task in order
___ Identify any potential obstacles and ways to overcome them
___ Clearly state your goals
___ Prepare a schedule and assign task deadlines

B. Discuss: In groups, talk about what the five characteristics of business objectives below mean. Give specific examples if you can. When you are finished, share your ideas with the class.

☞ Specific
☞ Measurable
☞ Attainable
☞ Relevant
☞ Timely

C. Focus: In terms of business goals, what point is the following question trying to make?

If you don't know where you're going, how will you know how to get there?

D. Read: Read the following article.

In business, strategic planning – a set of decisions an organization has to make about what to do, why to do it, and how to do it – is a management tool that helps an organization improve its overall performance. The aim is to define goals and objectives and develop strategies to reach them. All this must be done in the context of an ever-changing business environment.

Evaluating your organization's current situation is the best way to begin the strategic planning process. Figure out what you have to work with by analyzing your strengths and weaknesses. Then determine how you can capitalize on what you do well.

Once you've made a sound assessment, figure out where you want your organization to be. Articulate a clear vision in the form of a mission statement (a comprehensive statement of purpose) and determine the goals you want to achieve. You will also need to focus on the means of reaching your goals: how you will achieve results.

Goal measurement is another important step. To do this, you will need to establish benchmarks. Benchmarks are target levels of performance expressed in measurable terms and specified time frames, against which actual achievements are measured. Without these in place, it will be difficult to ascertain how much progress you have made over a given period of time.

When you develop a strategic plan, it is important to keep it as clear and brief as possible. If your plan has too many goals, you will be overwhelmed by the details of data collection and reporting. Ideally, strive to choose a limited number of broad goals that reflect multiple objectives.

E. Comprehension Check: Complete the sentences below **without** looking back at the article.

1. Strategic planning is a _____.

2. Strategic planning helps an organization _____
   _____.

3. The aim of strategic planning is to _____
   _____.

4. The best way to begin the strategic planning process is to _____
   _____.

5. It is important to articulate a clear vision in the form of a _____
   _____, which is a _____
   _____.

6. You also need to determine the _____ you want to achieve and the
   _____ of reaching them.

7. To measure goals, you will need _____, which are _____
   _____
   _____.

8. Be sure to keep your strategic plan _____ (expressed in few words).

F. Rethink: What could your company do better? What does it need to do? Why does it need to do these things? How can they be accomplished?

Section 4 ◆ Activity: Implementing Strategies

Directions*: Follow the steps below to implement a strategy. First, identify a competitive market (*e.g.,* mp3 players). Agree as a class. Then, in teams:*

1. Design a product with the aim of outselling the competition.

2. Set goals and objectives.

3. Sell your idea to your classmates and see if you can win them over.

4. Vote on choosing the best product (based on design and functionality).

5. (If time) Identify up to three more competitive markets and repeat the process.

♦ Presenting Ideas ♦

Section 1 ♦ Starting Point: Presentations

A. Warm Up: Match each type of business presentation on the left with its purpose on the right.

1. ___ **Persuade**   a. Help improve proficiency via specialized instruction and practice

2. ___ **Motivate**   b. Amuse and enliven

3. ___ **Train**   c. Provide facts about a topic

4. ___ **Stimulate**   d. Create enthusiasm and increase performance level for a project

5. ___ **Inform**   e. Convince your audience to accept an idea or take a specific action

6. ___ **Entertain**   f. Get people to think about a problem or situation

Do you have to give presentations at work? If you do, which types of presentation do you have to give the most often? Are there any types of presentation you have to give that are not listed above?

B. Group Work 1: Discuss the following questions.

1. Do you enjoy giving presentations? Explain.

2. What are your strengths and weaknesses as a presenter?

3. Can you think of anyone who is really good at giving presentations? Why do you think this person is such a good public speaker?

C. Group Work 2:

Every presentation has three major parts – an opening (beginning), a body (middle), and a closing (end). Below are specific functions of each one. Follow the example and write *opening* (O), *body* (B), or *closing* (C) on the line next to each function.

1. <u>C</u> Take questions (although you could do this during your presentation as well)

2. ___ Introduce the topic and grab the attention of your audience

3. ___ End with some final thoughts or remarks

4. ___ Preview the main points you will talk about

5. ___ Summarize all of your main points

6. ___ State your main points and provide supporting details

7. ___ Welcome your audience

8. ___ Thank your audience for attending

9. ___ Check the sequence of main points and the transitions between them

10. ___ Explain your purpose

Now put the functions of each part of a presentation in the order in which you would perform them. When you complete all three, you will have an outline for an effective business presentation.

Opening	**Body**	**Closing**
1. _____	5. _____	7. _____
2. _____	6. _____	8. _____
3. _____		9. _____
4. _____		10. _____

Section 2 ♦ Communication Strategies: ⊙ CD 1 track 17
Making a presentation

Part 1: Read, listen to, and say these sentences and phrases.

Welcoming

Thank you for being here today.
Thank you for taking the time to be here today.
It's good to see all of you here today.
Welcome to ___/I'd like to welcome you to ___.

Greeting

My name's ___. I'm the ___ (job) at ___ (company).

Introducing the subject

Today, I'm going to present/explain/talk about ___.
The subject/topic/focus of my presentation is ___.
I'm going to talk to you today about ___.
Today I'd like to focus on ___.

Stating the purpose

My aim/objective/purpose is (to) ___.
The purpose of this talk is to ___.
The reason I'm here today is ___.
I'm here today to ___.

Previewing points

I've divided my presentation into three parts. First, ___.
Then, ___. And finally, ___.

Sequencing

Let me begin/start by ___.
The first thing I'd like to talk about is ___.
Let's move on to my next point.
My second point is ___.
That brings me to my next point.
And now to my final/last point.

Summarizing

To summarize/sum up, ___.   In summary, ___.
In conclusion, ___.   As you can see, ___.

Inviting questions

Please hold any questions you (may) have until the end of my presentation.
(After previewing)

Please feel free to interrupt me at any time if you have (any) questions.
(After previewing)

If you have any questions, I'll be glad to answer them now.
(End of presentation)

Closing

Thank you for listening.
Thank you for your attention.

Part 2: Fill in the blanks with the phrases in **bold** type. When you are finished, read the presentation. Take turns reading all three parts with your partner.

⊙ CD 1 track 18

First   Today, I'm going to talk about   My objective is to
Thank you for taking the time
finally   I've divided my presentation   My name's   Then

_____ to be here today. _____
Meredith Flannery. I'm the product manager at PhotoStar. _____
_____ our new digital superzoom camera, the X8. _____
_____ demonstrate how our camera is the best in its
class. _____ into three parts.
_____, I'll talk about the design. _____ I'll show you
some of its features. And _____, I'll highlight how it compares to
cameras from our competitors.

let's move on to my next point   That brings me to
Let me start by   Now that I've told you about

_____ talking about the design. The X8 has an all-plastic
body with a very solid feel. It's also heavy enough to help you hold the camera
steady. The X8 also . . .
_____ the design, _____
_____: features. The X8 has a powerful optical zoom lens and many
shooting modes. In addition, it . . .

_____ my last point: how it compares to our competitors' products. The first thing you'll notice is the price. It's cheaper than any other camera of its kind on the market today. And . . .

**As you can see   Thank you for your attention   summarize
I'll be glad to answer them now**

To _____, I talked about the design and features of our new X8 camera and how it compares to other cameras of its kind on the market today. We're very proud of our development team. They did a great job with this model. It's going to be hard to top! _____, we are confident that you will be completely satisfied if you decide to purchase an X8 – which I hope you do. _____.

If you have any questions, _____.

Part 3: Work with a partner. Use the information below to write the opening of a presentation.

Name: (*your own)   *Product*: New laptop – T3X

Job: Sales manager   *Purpose*: Superior product

Company: Computer store   *Points*: Design, features, comparison

Part 4: Use the information below to write the body of a presentation.

Design: Very light, portable (easy to carry around)

Features: Great video/graphics card, fast mobile processor, large system drive, lots of memory

Comparison: Cheaper, lighter, larger screen (versus other similar products available on the market)

Part 5: Write the closing of a presentation.

Be sure to (1) summarize by restating the points you made, (2) make some closing remarks, (3) thank your audience for their attention, and (4) invite questions.

Part 6: Read your complete presentation to each other. Then practice delivering your presentation in front of the class.

Section 3 ♦ Reading: Presentation preparation

A. Activate: What makes an effective presentation? Make a list with a partner.

```



```

B. Focus:

Here are some good questions to ask yourself when preparing a presentation. Write the words on the lines

Audience   Content   Sources   Purpose
Place   Topic   Visual aids   Wording

1. _____ Why am I making this presentation?

2. _____ What is this presentation about?

3. _____ What information do I need to include?

4. _____ Do I have access to a lot of useful information?

5. _____ Where am I giving this presentation? What equipment is available? What is the size of the room and how is it arranged?

6. _____ Who am I speaking to? How many people will there be? Is my topic relevant and interesting for them? What do they need? How do they feel about the topic? How much do they know already?

7. _____ How should I phrase my key points so that I can communicate them clearly and effectively?

8. _____ Have I chosen the most effective graphs, charts, slides, or handouts to clarify, emphasize, and dramatize my verbal information?

C. Read: Read the following article.

How can I deliver my speech in a professional manner? This is another good question you need to ask yourself while you are preparing your presentation. Delivering a presentation can be a daunting affair. It is not easy to speak in front of other people. But, with some helpful guidance, you can deliver a successful speech that will be remembered for all the right reasons.

More than the words you actually say, voice quality and visual characteristics are what people evaluate you on when you give a presentation. So, it is critical that you speak slowly, clearly, and loudly. Articulate each word properly, avoid using fillers (*e.g.,* "um" and "uh"), and speak loudly enough so that the people in the back row don't have to strain to hear you. Furthermore, do not speak in a monotone like a robot (which is often the result of committing your presentation to memory and focusing your attention solely on recall, or from reading directly from your notes too much). Use stress (loudness) and intonation to emphasize your main points. And do what you can to avoid any awkward moments of silence.

Just as your voice can project confidence or fear, your body language reflects how you feel. Make sure you stand up straight with your head erect. You also should try to keep your hands at your side, unless you are using gestures to emphasize or communicate a point. And when you are standing still, keep your feet slightly apart to steady yourself.

In addition to good posture, make sure that you use appropriate facial expressions. Smile to establish a rapport with your audience and use your face to convey different emotions throughout your presentation. Also, make eye contact with everyone in the room, not just the people in the front row. This will make each person in attendance feel that they are included.

If you use visual aids, be sure to speak to the audience – not to the screen, board, or flipchart. In other words, do not turn your back on your audience when referring to them. Stand to the side of your visual aid, facing the audience instead. If you are using a pointer, do not wave it around or bang it on the lectern or table. It is not a toy. Use it when you need it, and put it down when you do not.

Also, be careful about the time. Stick to what you are allotted. It is better to finish early or right on schedule than it is to continue beyond what is expected of you.

Finally, practice, practice, practice. Read your presentation over several times silently in a location that is quiet and free from distractions. Then try reading your presentation aloud a few times. You can practice your delivery in front of a mirror. This will help you to observe your posture, gestures, and facial expressions. Also, you can read your presentation into a voice recorder or in front of a video camera and then listen to or watch yourself. This will help you note errors and what needs to be improved. You can also read your presentation to family members or friends. They can provide you with some honest feedback.

D. Comprehension Check: Write true (**T**) or false (**F**) next to each statement about giving a presentation. If the statement is false, rewrite it to make it true.

1. ___ The words you actually say are more important than voice quality and visual characteristics.
2. ___ Speaking slowly, clearly, and loudly is very important.
3. ___ Speak in a monotone, being sure not to use inflection to emphasize your main points.
4. ___ Avoid any awkward moments of silence.
5. ___ Body language reflects how you feel about yourself.
6. ___ Don't rest your hands on the lectern.
7. ___ Smile to establish rapport with your audience.
8. ___ Practicing silently is not helpful.
9. ___ Speak to your visual aids, not to your audience.
10. ___ Continuing beyond your allotted time is never a problem.

E. Anxiety: Most people get nervous before they have to give a presentation. Below is a list of tips for helping you reduce anxiety. Try to elaborate what each one means.

☞ Organize your thoughts

☞ Practice – standing up and using your visual aids

☞ Know the room (size and arrangement)

☞ Focus on relaxing

☞ Visualize yourself speaking

☞ Understand that people want you to succeed

☞ Don't admit or apologize for being nervous

☞ Concentrate on your message – not the medium

☞ Move around the room

☞ Gain experience

F. Visual Aids: Why and when should you use visual aids? Put a ✔ next to the ones you should do and an ✗ next to the ones you should not. Be prepared to explain your answers.

1. ___ to impress your audience with overwhelming detail or animation
2. ___ to stimulate interest
3. ___ to focus the audience's attention
4. ___ to reduce the amount of speaking time
5. ___ to illustrate factors that are hard to visualize
6. ___ to present simple ideas that are easily stated
7. ___ to reinforce your verbal message
8. ___ to avoid interaction with your audience

Now, just as you did in the previous section, try to say more about each of the visual aid tips below.

☞   Use images sparingly

☞   Make slides pictorial

☞   Present one key point per slide

☞   Make text and numbers legible

☞   Use color carefully

☞   Make visuals big enough to see

☞   Graph data

☞   Make pictures and diagrams easy to see

☞   Avoid unnecessary images

☞   Use animation sparingly

Now make a list of tips for creating better images with presentation software. Draw on your own experience.

F. Rethink:

What will you make sure to do the next time you have to give a presentation?

Section 4 ♦ Activity: Give a presentation

Directions*:* Prepare a business presentation about one of the following subjects.

☞   A company (your own or one you admire and want to know more about)

☞   A person (*e.g.* a leader who is having a big impact on business today)

☞   A product or service

☞   A current business news item or issue

For help, follow the outline in Starting Point and the examples in Communication Strategies. You may use visual aids if you want to.

When you're finished, give your presentation. Your time limit will be **5 minutes**.

As you are listening to your classmates give their presentations, take notes and give feedback about:

1. *Delivery*

☞   Eye contact

☞   Voice quality – clarity, volume, fillers, inflection (monotone)

☞   Posture, gestures, and facial expressions

☞   Visual aids (if any)

2. *Content*

☞   Opening

☞   Body (organization of points)

☞   Closing

Whose presentation did you like? Why?

◆ Expressing Opinions ◆

Section 1 ◆ Starting Point: Quotations

A. Warm Up: Discuss the following questions with a partner.

1. Are you comfortable expressing your opinions at work? Why or why not?
2. Have you ever regretted expressing your opinion at work? If so, what happened?
3. Have you ever wanted to express your opinion at work but were afraid to do so or held back? If so, why?

B. Group Work: Do you agree or disagree with the following quotations? Discuss with another pair and provide explanations for your responses.

1. The only way to know how customers see your business is to look at it through their eyes.
   – *Daniel R. Scroggin, Chief Executive Officer (CEO) of TGI Fridays Inc.*

2. There are no secrets to success. It is the result of preparation, hard work, and learning from failure.
   – *Colin Powell, U.S. soldier and statesman*

3. People are definitely a company's greatest asset. It doesn't make any difference whether the product is cars or cosmetics. A company is only as good as the people it keeps.
   – *Mary Kay Ash, founder of Mary Kay Cosmetics*

4. Management is nothing more than motivating other people.
   – *Lee Iacocca, former chairman of Chrysler Corporation*

5. Meetings are indispensable when you don't want to achieve anything.
   – *John Kenneth Galbraith, American diplomat, economist, and writer*

6. In business, you don't get what you deserve, you get what you negotiate.
   – *Chester L. Karrass, negotiating seminar leader and consultant*

7. Few things are the same everywhere, and almost no (business) strategy works well globally.
   – *David Ricks, author*

8. If you can dream it, you can do it.
   – *Walt Disney, filmmaker and animator*

C. As a Class:

Discuss the following questions.

1. Which quotation do you like best? Why?

2. Can you think of any other famous (business) quotations? How about popular sayings in your culture?

3. What's the purpose of quotations? How are they useful in business?

Section 2 ♦ Communication Strategies: ⊙ CD 1 track 19
Expressing Opinions

Part 1: Read, listen to, and say these sentences and phrases.

Asking for opinions

What do you think (about) ___?
What are your thoughts on ___?
What's your view/take on ___?
What do you make of this?
How do you feel (about this)?
Don't you agree/think so?

Stating your opinion

I believe that ___.
If you ask me, ___.
It's (pretty) clear/obvious that ___.
As I see it, ___.
It seems ___.
As far as I'm concerned, ___.
From my perspective, ___.
You might not agree with me, but ___.

Agreeing

I totally/completely agree with you.
I couldn't agree (with you) more.
I'm sure/convinced that ___.
I think so too.
We see eye to eye (on this).
You're absolutely right.
Absolutely./Certainly.
That's for sure.

Disagreeing

I see what you mean, but ___.
I can see where you're coming from, but ___.
That may be true, but ___.
Well, it depends.
I'm not so sure about that.
I'm not convinced that ___.
Do you really think so?
I don't believe that ___.
I totally disagree with you.
I couldn't disagree (with you) more.

Part 2: Fill in the blanks with the phrases in **bold** type. When you are finished, read the dialogs with a partner. Then switch roles and read the dialogs again.

⊙ CD 1 track 20

You may be right   What are your thoughts on
I'm not convinced that   It's pretty clear

A: _____ the upcoming merger?

B: _____ that a lot of people are going to lose their jobs.

A: _____, but I think a lot of people will be promoted, too.

B: Good point, but _____ the benefits will outweigh the costs.

I totally agree with you   What's your take on this?
If you ask me   I can see where you're coming from

A: _____, I think we should hire some part-time employees to help us finish this project. _____?

B: _____, but I don't think Human Resources would approve of this, especially in light of our budget.

A: As far as I'm concerned, getting the job done on time is more important than how much it will cost.

B: _____, but I think we're on our own this time.

what you mean   from my perspective   Don't you think so
I'm not so sure about that   it seems   That may be true
Can you give me an example

A: I know that poverty is a serious issue, but some protesters go a little too far sometimes. _____?

B: Well, _____ the protesters want to blame someone, and the main targets are usually world leaders or big companies.

A: Some world leaders I can understand, but _____, more than a few companies bring wealth, power, and even opportunity to countries that are less well off.

B: _____, but far too many people still live in areas that have been left behind.

A: I see _____, but isn't the attainment of a country's needs supposed to be the job of government?

C: _____. Many governments, especially in the developing world, fail to meet expectations. As a result of this failure, big companies often find themselves playing a supporting role.

A: Really? _____?

C: I believe Company Y has done rural development work in Haiti, and I think Company X provides educational programs in Mali.

Part 3: With a partner, create and practice a dialog based on the following flow chart. Use business communication strategies from this chapter to help you. When you are finished, switch roles. Create and practice a similar dialog **without** using the flow chart.

A1: Greet your partner and ask for an opinion about a business or current events topic.

B1: State your opinion about the topic.

A2: Clarify (ask for more details).

B2: State your opinion in more depth.

A3: Agree or disagree (depending on how you feel).

B3: Ask for repetition.

A4: Repeat what you said, but in more depth this time.

B4: Agree or disagree (depending on how you feel).

A5: Respond as necessary, then ask for an opinion about a similar (related) business or current events topic.

B5: State your opinion about the topic.

A6: Agree or disagree (depending on how you feel).

B6: Say more about your opinion, to include agreeing or disagreeing with your partner.

A7: Use a rejoinder and follow-up question (about your partner's opinion).

B7: Respond to your partner.

Part 4: Switch partners. Complete the statements below.

(A) Say your sentences to your partner. Ask if she or he agrees or disagrees with you. Give reasons for your opinions.

1. I think _____ would be the best company to work for (in this country).

3. It's pretty clear that _____ is the worst fast food chain.

5. It seems as if _____ would be a great job to have.

7. From my perspective, _____ is the toughest thing most managers have to deal with.

9. It's obvious that _____ would be the most challenging part of being an entrepreneur.

11. Obviously, _____ was the most significant technological innovation of the 20th century.

(B) Say your sentences to your partner. Ask if s/he agrees or disagrees with you. Give reasons for your opinions.

2. I believe _____ will overtake the United States as the world's biggest economy one day.

4. If you ask me, _____ is the most influential business leader in the world.

6. You might not agree with me, but _____ would be a good company to invest in.

8. As far as I'm concerned, _____ is the best car on the market.

10. Clearly, _____ is the most important piece of advice you can give to someone looking for a new job.

12. I feel that _____ is an alternative to fossil fuel and a sustainable energy source.

Part 5: Do you agree or disagree with the following statements? Why? Discuss with a partner.

   (A) Read the following statements to your partner. Ask for your partner's opinion about each one.

   1. The customer is always right.

   3. Globalization helps improve the quality of life for people around the world.

   5. Wireless innovation (*e.g.* cell phones and PDAs) leads to poor public manners.

   7. The negative impact of outsourcing on economies and employment is greatly exaggerated.

   9. Downloading copyrighted music from peer-to-peer networks should be legal.

   11. Well-known brand names (*e.g.* Coca-Cola or Google) help create trust in the minds of consumers.

   (B) Read the following statements to your partner. Ask for your partner's opinion about each one.

   2. Advertising to young children is unethical.

   4. Creativity and imagination are more important than science and technology in developing new products.

   6. Customers should refrain from buying any goods made by slave labor.

   8. Investors should take the same approach to buying shares that they would if they were buying a business.

   10. Business and religion should never be mixed – no matter where you are doing business in the world.

   12. Companies should be required to give back to communities.

Part 6: With a partner, write several opinions about business or current events in the space below. Using the business communication strategies, state your opinions to one another. Then find new partners and see if they agree or disagree with you.

Section 3 ◆ Reading: CEO Salaries

CEO compensation is a very controversial issue. With the following article and exercises, you will have an opportunity to examine this issue and express your opinions about it.

A. Activate: Read the statements in the chart. Do you agree or disagree with them? Put a check in either of the first two columns. After you read the article, see if you still feel the same way and put a check in either of the last two columns.

Before you read			After you read	
Agree	Disagree		Agree	Disagree
		CEOs are overpaid.		
		It is difficult to make a meaningful comparison between the value of two different jobs, particularly in terms of compensation.		
		Business and politics don't mix.		

B. Discuss: With a partner, discuss the statements and your responses. Provide reasons for your opinions.

C. Focus: What do you already know about the issue of CEO compensation? What would you like to know about this topic? Write three questions you would like the article to answer.

1.

2.

3.

D. Read: After you read each paragraph, write the main idea on the lines below it.

Are CEOs overpaid? That's debatable.

Did you know that the CEOs of a Standard & Poor's 500 company made an average of nearly $15 million in total compensation in 2006? This compensation includes an annual salary, bonuses, stock option gains, and various other executive benefits. In contrast, the average, middle-class American was paid approximately $45,000 that same year. That means chief executive pay was roughly 330 times that of the average worker.

Main idea: _____

_____

Needless to say, many people feel that CEOs are overpaid. Too much power, inattentive boards of directors, conflicts of interest by compensation consultants, and stock options, among others, have all been cited as potential causes of over-payment. However, it is difficult to determine the relative value of the individuals in a job. What is the appropriate compensation for a CEO of a large American company who has advanced degrees from the top business schools in the world, works 70 or more hours per week, and has held many important positions with high levels of responsibility over the years?

Main idea: _____

_____

A large part of the problem lies in measuring worker pay. A good portrayal of how much the average American worker is paid for their work would include wage or salary, overtime pay, bonuses, tips, commissions, stock-based compensation, and hiring and retention bonuses, and various benefits. Unfortunately, the data used in measuring worker pay is far from comprehensive. In addition, most of us believe that different jobs with different educational requirements and different levels of responsibility should be paid differently, but we don't know or agree on how differently. So how do we make a meaningful comparison between any two jobs, including those of the average worker and a CEO?

Main idea: _____

_____

Clearly, fixing the problem will not entail measuring the wrong things and then misinterpreting flawed calculations. This will likely only lead to misguided legislation, and might also encourage big shareholders and their advisors to begin bullying companies into change using arbitrary standards. Instead, we need to stay focused on the real problem of executive pay practices. Perhaps accurate disclosure of pay will allow us to identify egregious practices and apply pressure to help remedy the situation.

Main idea: _____

_____

E. Comprehension Check: Are the following statements True (T) or False (F)? Rewrite the false statements to make them true.

_____ 1. CEOs are paid a lot more than the average worker in the United States.

_____ 2. Many Americans feel that CEOs are paid too much for the job they do.

_____ 3. Measuring worker pay should focus only on wages and overtime.

_____ 4. The data for determining worker pay is comprehensive.

_____ 5. Most people believe that different jobs with different educational requirements and different levels of responsibility should be paid differently, but there is no consensus on what "differently" means.

_____ 6. Accurate disclosure of pay will not likely allow us to identify egregious practices and apply pressure to help remedy the situation.

F. Rethink: Read the statements in Part A again. Decide whether you agree or disagree with them after reading the article. State reasons for your opinions. Then agree or disagree with the statements below. Discuss your opinions with a partner.

1. Most CEOs have an incredibly demanding job and earn the money they make.

2. Compensation for CEOs should be based on how a company performs.

3. When a company does well, the wealth should be proportionately shared with all stockholders.

4. The trend in excessive executive pay will not be reversed anytime soon.

Section 4 ◆ Activity: Case studies

Directions: With a partner, read the case studies below and answer the questions that follow.

Case Study 1

You are the newly appointed CEO of a large snack food corporation. Some of the more serious challenges you face include disappointing sales and earnings, increased competition, several failed new product launches[1], and sudden departures of key senior executives. In the midst of your turn-around efforts[2], you are faced with a new challenge: rapidly escalating[3] public attention to the obesity[4] epidemic[5] in the United States, and increasingly in the global marketplace. Given the enormous[6] health, policy, and economic implications of this trend, the opportunities and responsibilities of major players in the food business, including yourself, are under examination by the media, politicians, and various non-governmental organizations.

What should the role of business, and of your corporation, be in regard to such a complex social, ethical, and economic issue in a competitive market environment? And, in a world of "bottom line" calculations, how do you measure the varied potential costs and benefits of your actions?

What's your take on this? What are you going to do? Have a classmate play devil's advocate[7] and debate this. Be sure to use the business communication strategies to help you express your opinion.

[1] **product launch**: introduction of a product to the public or to a market

[2] **turn-around efforts**: efforts made to improve something on the decline

[3] **escalating**: increasing

[4] **obesity**: increased body weight caused by excessive accumulation of fat

[5] **epidemic**: a rapid spread, growth, or development

[6] **enormous**: very large

[7] **devil's advocate**: one who argues against a cause or position simply for the sake of argument

Case Study 2

Many residents and local merchants[1] are opposed to the development of a large discount department store[2] outlet[3] in their neighborhood. The residents and merchants argue that the development and store will generate excessive noise and traffic, as well as negatively affect local 'mom and pop'[4] businesses. The discount department store, however, insists that they try to take a community approach, and will not contribute to the decline of the downtown retail centers. Instead, they will help lower the cost of living to lower-income earners. The debate among retailers, local residents, the city council, and the discount department store captures some of the tumult[5] around the role of multinational corporations in the global economy and their effects on societies and the environment.

What are your thoughts on this? Take sides or assign roles and debate this with your classmates. Be sure to use the business communication strategies to help you express your opinion.

[1] **merchants**: shopkeepers

[2] **discount department store**: similar to department stores, but the prices are lower and the goods are usually cheaper in quality

[3] **outlet**: a store that sells the goods of a particular manufacturer or wholesaler

[4] **mom and pop**: a small business that is typically owned and run by members of a family

[5] **tumult**: disorderly commotion or disturbance

♦ Considering Options and Choices ♦

Section 1 ♦ Starting Point: Options and choices

A. Warm Up: Discuss the following questions with a partner.

When was the last time you had to consider several options or choices and make an important decision at work?

☞   What did you have to consider in that situation?

☞   What was at stake?

☞   What was the outcome?

☞   Were you pleased with the results?

☞   In hindsight, is there anything you would have done differently? Why or why not?

B. Group Work 1: Which would you choose? Give reasons for your choices.

Would you rather . . .

1. Have a great job that you really like but doesn't pay very well, or have a boring, unsatisfying job that pays very well?

2. Work for a well-known organization, insuring job security, or have your own business, which would be very risky but potentially very profitable?

3. Go back to school full-time for a higher degree so that you can get a better job later (which would require sacrificing time and money) or stay in your current job and slowly work your way up in the organization?

C. Group Work 2: Answer the following hypothetical questions. Give reasons for your answers.

1. If you could change one thing about your job, what would it be?

2. If you could work for any company in the world, who would you want to work for?

3. If you could work in any city in the world, where would you want to work?

4. If you could have dinner with any prominent business leader in the world, who would it be? What would you want to talk about?

5. If you could speak any three languages that you do not speak now, what languages would you want to speak? Why?

Section 2 ◆ Communication Strategies: ⊙ CD 2 track 1
Choosing between options

Part 1: Read, listen to, and say these sentences and phrases.

Suggesting and recommending

Why don't you ____?
What/How about ____?
Perhaps you could ____.
Let's ____.
If I were you, ____.
I think we should ____.
It might be a good idea to ____.
I (strongly) suggest/recommend ____.

Asking for a recommendation

Do you have any recommendations?
What do you recommend/suggest?
What do you think we should do?
What's our best option (at this point)?

Thinking it over

I need some time to think about that.
I'll think it over and get back to you.

Asking someone to think it over

Mull it over.
Give it some thought.

Hypothesizing

If you were me/in my shoes, what would you do?
What if ____?
What would you do if ____?
Suppose [*situation]. Would you be willing to ____?

Part 2: Fill in the blanks with the phrases in **bold** type. When you are finished, read the dialogs with a partner. Then switch roles and read the dialogs again.

⊙ CD 2 track 2

It might be a good idea   What do you think
Give it some thought

A: Shares in our company have fallen 10% over the last three months.

B: I know. _____ we should do?

A: _____ to call an emergency meeting.

B: But I don't want people to panic. It might just be a temporary setback.

A: _____. It sure wouldn't hurt.

What if   Do you have any recommendations
I think we   Why don't we

A: We need to make a decision about where to hold the conference this year. _____?

B: _____ have it at the Convention Center again?

A: I'd love to, but it's already reserved for the dates we want.

B: _____ we changed the dates?

A: We can't. Too many people have already made plans for that weekend.

B: _____ should make a list of all the possible places, and then call to see which ones can work with us.

A: Good idea.

could   If I were you   I'll think it over
Perhaps you could   If you were me

A: I've gotten a lot of complaints about Marcelo lately. He seems to be increasingly uncooperative and insubordinate. _____, what would you do?

B: _____, I'd call him into your office and talk to him.

A: I've tried that, but apparently it didn't work very well.

B: _____ put him on probation. He might take you more seriously that way.

A: That's not a bad idea.

B: You _____ also fire him. It's not like he hasn't had any warnings.

A: True. _____ this afternoon. Let's talk again later.

Part 3: With a partner, create and practice a dialog based on the following flow chart. Use business communication strategies from this chapter to help you. When you are finished, switch roles. Create and practice the same dialog.

A1: You want to invest your money, but you are not sure what to do. Ask for a recommendation.

B1: Suggest investing in real estate.

A2: Ask why.

B2: Give reasons for your suggestion.

A3: Ask for another recommendation.

B3: Suggest investing in stocks.

A4: Express your concern about the risks.

B4: Suggest investing in mutual funds – less risk.

A5: Say that you will think this over.

B5: Recommend stocks again – emphasize that the potential return is greater than with mutual funds.

A6: Say that you will think about this too.

Spec Data	X352	M788	R196
Text quality	★ ★ ★	★ ★ ★ ★	★ ★ ★ ★ ★
Photo quality	★ ★	★ ★ ★ ★	★ ★ ★ ★ ★
Speed	★	★ ★ ★	★ ★ ★ ★ ★
Scans/Faxes	No	No	Yes
Price	$900	$2,000	$3,100

Ratings: ★★★★★ Excellent, ★★★★ Very good, ★★★ Good, ★★ Average, ★ Poor

A1: Say that your department needs a new laser printer. Ask for a recommendation.

B1: Suggest that your partner check online.

A2: Say that you've done that already. Show your partner the spec data and ask what s/he thinks.

B2: Tell your partner what you think the most important feature is.

A3: Respond to your partner.

                                              B3: Make a statement about the needs of your department.

A4: Respond to your partner.

                                              B4: Ask if price is an issue.

A5: Say you're not sure at this point.

                                              B5: Recommend a printer based on the needs of your department.

A6: Respond to your partner.

                                              B6: Ask when a decision has to be made.

A7: Say that you have to make a recommendation by the end of next week.

                                              B7: Tell your partner that she or he has some time to think it over.

Part 4: Group role play

Food Barn Inc. plans to introduce one of the following products next year. All of them will try to compete with the most successful brands in their respective markets.

🍽 A cola soft drink

🍽 A gourmet potato chip that uses all natural ingredients

🍽 A healthy breakfast cereal with fruits and nuts

🍽 A alcohol-free, spearmint-flavored mouthwash

🍽 A teriyaki steak sauce for dipping and marinating

Consider each option – weighing its potential strengths and weaknesses against the leading brands – and recommend one item for production. Use hypothetical ("if") questions to make predictions about the future performance of each product.

Part 4: If you had a choice, which of the following employee benefit plans would you prefer? Give reasons for your answers.

1. Employee stock ownership plan

This is a trust which acts as a retirement plan by making the organization's employees partial owners. Contributions are made by the employer. But unlike other retirement plans, this one requires that the contributions must be invested in the company's stock. The main benefit for the employees is the ability to share in the company's success.

2. Stock option plan

This grants employees the right to buy company stock at a specified price during a specified period once the option has vested (*i.e.* the employee has the right of ownership). It works like this: If an employee gets an option on 1000 shares at $100 and the stock price goes up to $200, the employee can "exercise" the option and buy those 1000 shares at $100 each, sell them on the market for $200 each, and keep the difference.

3. Employee stock purchase plan

Like a stock option plan, this gives employees the chance to buy stock, usually through payroll deductions over a specified "offering period" (usually 3 to 27 months). The price of the stock is usually discounted up to 15% from the market price. As with a stock option, after acquiring the stock the employee can sell it for a quick profit or hold onto it for a while. Unlike stock options, however, the discounted price built into most of these plans means that employees can profit even if the stock price has gone down since the grant date.

4. 401(k) plan

This is a retirement plan that is designed to provide the employee with a diversified portfolio of investments. The employees can choose from several or more options for investments, and the company may make a matching contribution.

Section 3 ◆ Reading: Decision trees

How do you select the best course of action in situations where you face uncertainty? With the following exercises and article, you will have an opportunity to examine this question.

A. Activate: Read the questions below and think about your answers.

1. As a consumer, do you like having a lot of choices when you go shopping?
2. Have you ever felt that you had too many choices, to the point where you simply couldn't make a decision?
3. Do you think too much choice hinders your motivation to buy something?
4. Have you ever been overwhelmed by choices in other areas of your life?

B. Discuss: In a group, discuss your answers to the questions above. See if you've had similar experiences.

C. Focus: What do you have to consider in the following situations? What can you do to insure that you make the right decisions?

1. You want to apply for a new job.
2. You want to buy a house or an apartment.
3. You want to start your own business.

D. Read: Read the following article.

When faced with more than one course of action in an important business situation, you need to be able to make an informed choice with confidence. One tool to help you do this is a decision tree, a graphic illustration of how alternative solutions lead to various possibilities. It is a decision support tool that helps you clearly see the implications (*i.e.* risks and rewards) that certain choices have for the future. Below is a simple example:

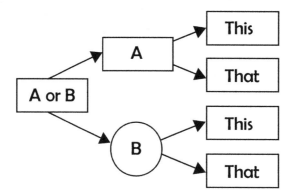

Start with a decision that needs to be made. In this case, you would ask yourself which option is better: A or B. If A, then you have the possibility of "this" or "that" happening. The same holds true for B. You then keep branching out and considering results until you reach your goal. Each time you go further out along the branches, carefully evaluate each possibility with as much data and support as you can.

In order to make the decision tree visually clear, you can use circles to denote decisions that will yield uncertain or potentially undesirable results. In the example above, you would feel more certain about choosing A than you would be choosing B.

Decision trees help you examine a situation while considering all potentialities in the process. The framework of a decision tree allows you to quantify the values of outcomes and the probabilities of achieving them. It is an invaluable tool for helping you reach the goal you set for yourself.

E. Comprehension Check: answer the following questions **without** looking back at the article.

☞   What is a decision tree?

☞   What does a decision tree help you do?

☞   How does a decision tree work? Explain by drawing.

F. Rethink: How can decision trees help you at work? Can you see their practical application?

Section 4 ♦ Activity: Application

Directions*:* Work with a partner.

Part 1: Make a decision tree for the following situation:

Choose a company that you want to invest in. Consider:

1. Its performance over the past few years (good, moderate, bad)
2. Its long-term potential (good, moderate, bad)
3. Your knowledge of, feelings about, and belief in their products or services (strong, moderate, weak)
4. Your aversion to risk (strong, moderate, weak)

Each time you select "good" or strong," you will move on to the next point of consideration. Whenever you select "moderate," "bad," or "weak," you need to examine the facts or your feelings, and decide whether investing in the company is a good idea or not.

Part 2: Now make a decision tree for a problematic or challenging situation at work. What is the best course of action? Why?

◆ **Making Decisions** ◆

Section 1 ◆ Starting Point: Leadership

A. Warm Up: Brainstorm in the boxes below.

Part 1: What skills must team leaders possess? Add to the list below.

> Oral communication (including listening)
> Delegating
> Managing time and stress

Part 2: Can you think of any famous CEOs who possess these outstanding leadership skills?

Who do you think is the most outstanding leader from the list above?

B. Group Work 1: Discuss the following questions.

1. Do you think leaders are born or made?

2. What personal characteristics help define great leaders?

3. Are there any differences between men and women as leaders? Who would you rather work for? Why?

C. Group Work 2: Evaluate your colleagues.

1. What are the strengths of your company's leadership team (*i.e.* executive officers)?

2. What are the strengths of your team manager?

3. Who do you think are the emerging leaders in your company?

D. As a Class: Discuss the following question.

Are you (or would you be) a good leader? Why or why not?

Section 2 ◆ Communication Strategies: Making Decisions

⊙ CD 2 track 3

Part 1: Read, listen to, and say these sentences and phrases.

Keeping to the point

Let's not get sidetracked.
Let's stay focused on ____.
Let's stick to ____.
Let's not lose sight of ____.

Referring to time

We're running out of time.
We're almost out of time.
We're spending too much time on ____.
We can't spend any more time on ____.

Calling for a decision

Are we ready to make a decision?
I think it's time to make a decision.

Establishing a consensus

Does everyone agree that _____?
Is everyone in agreement?
We all agree that _____, right?
Everyone thinks/feels that _____, right?

Asking about objections

Are there any objections?
Does anyone object to _____?

Delaying a decision

We need more time to think about this.
We should hold off until _____.
We should postpone the decision until _____.
We can't make a final decision until _____.

Confirming a decision

So, we've decided to _____, right?
Just to be clear, we're going to _____, right?

Part 2: Fill in the blanks with the phrases in **bold** type. When you are finished, read
the dialogs with a partner. Then switch roles and read the dialogs again.

⊙ CD 2 track 4

Does everyone agree that   sidetracked   just to be clear
we're running out of time   Are we ready
Let's stay focused on   objections

A: _____ why we're here today – which PR
firm we want to work with. Let's not get _____.

B: Actually, I think _____.

A: True. We've only got about ten more minutes. _____
to make a decision?

B: I think so.

A: _____ Johnson and Schwartz is our best bet?

All: Yes.

A: Are there any _____? No? Good. So, _____
_____, we've ruled out the other firms, right?

we should postpone the decision until   **We all agree that**
We're spending way too much time   **Does anyone object to this**   **Let's not**
lose sight of   **We'd better**   **out of time**

A: _____ talking about something

that's not really relevant. _____ why we're

having this meeting.

A: *[Later]* We're almost _____.

_____ make a decision. _____

we should pursue legal action, right?

B: No. I definitely don't agree.

A: What are you concerned about?

B: I don't think our case is strong enough.

A: I see. Well, perhaps _____ we do

some more research.

B: I think we should talk to our lawyers and see what they have to say.

A: Fair enough. _____?

Part 3: With a partner, create and practice a dialog based on the following flow chart. Use business communication strategies from this chapter to help you. When you're finished, switch roles. Create and practice the same dialog.

A1: Ask your partner to keep to the point. Then ask them to focus on the reason for the meeting – downsizing your organization.

B1: Apologize to your partner (for lack of focus).

A2: Refer to time.

B2: Respond to your partner.

A3: Call for a decision.

B3: Respond to your partner.

A4: Establish a consensus with your partner in favor of downsizing.

B4: Object by citing reasons why it would be a bad idea.

A5: Respond to your partner.

B5: Suggest delaying the decision.

A6: Refer to time – need to make a decision very soon.

B6: Reiterate your objection(s).

A7: Agree to a delay, but emphasize the limited amount of time.

B7: Respond to your partner.

Part 4: Put the following steps of the decision-making process in order from 1 (first) to 8 (last).

___ Monitor implementation of the plan
___ Examine potential causes for the situation
___ Verify whether or not the situation has been dealt with effectively
_1_ Define the situation
___ Agree upon an approach to deal with the situation
___ Reflect on the situation after it has been dealt with
___ Plan the implementation of the best approach (to include prioritizing tasks)
___ Think about different ways to deal with the situation

Check your order by writing the steps of the decision-making process on the lines above their corresponding questions. Follow the example.

1. *Define the situation*
   _____
   Questions: What is going on? When did it start? Who is it affecting?

2. _____
   Questions: Why is it happening? What could possibly be behind this?

3. _____
   Question: What are our options (at this point)?

4. _____
   Question: What is the best way to handle this situation?

5. _____
   Questions: What is the goal? What steps need to be taken to reach this goal? What resources are required? How long will it take?

6. _____
   Questions: Is everything going as expected? Are we on schedule?

7. _____
   Question: Did everything work out as planned?

8. _____
   Question: What changes should be made to avoid this type of situation in the future?

Part 5: Work in groups of three or four. Each person in your group must think of one situation that requires decision making. This can be a current or past situation at work or a situation that a famous organization has to deal with (or had to deal with) and must make (or had to make) a decision about. Clearly define the situation and identify the causes for it before you begin. When everyone is finished, pretend you are in a meeting and use role play to act out each decision-making process. The person who thought of the situation is the leader in each role play.

Section 3 ♦ Reading: Six Thinking Hats – Edward de Bono

Seeing things from different perspectives is a good idea in strategy formation or complex decision-making processes. With the following exercises and article, you will have an opportunity to examine this issue and express your opinions about it.

A. Activate: Examine the following decision-making models and think about their usefulness:

1. **Cost-benefit analysis**   Weigh total expected benefits (pros) versus the expected costs (cons)
2. **Force-field analysis**   Analyze forces that either drive or hinder movement toward a goal
3. **Paired-comparison analysis**   Examine different options relative to each other
4. **Pareto analysis**   Select a limited number of tasks that produces the most significant overall effect
5. **PMI (Plus/Minus/Implications)**   Check to see if a course of action is going to improve a situation
6. **Satisficing**   Select the first option that meets a given need or select the option that seems to address most needs rather than the "optimal" solution
7. **Scenario analysis**   Analyze possible future events
8. **SWOT analysis**   Evaluate Strengths, Weaknesses, Opportunities and Threats with respect to desired goal

Now discuss the following questions with a partner.

1. Have you ever used any of these models (or an approximation of them) at work or in your personal life? Answer via examples.

2. Can you think of an example of the application of each model at work or in the business world?

B. Think: Put a check next to the strategies that you've used to make difficult decisions at work.

____ Compare current situation with similar situations from the past and identify lessons learned.

____ Redefine a complex situation by seeing it as a series of steps.

____ Stimulate a rigorous debate among all people involved in the situation.

____ Other(s):_____.

Which of these do you think is the most effective? Why?

C. Focus: Discuss the following questions in groups. Then share with the class.

Are you able to look at a problem or situation from different points of view? Why is this important? Answer these questions by citing an example of a situation at work or school.

D. Read: Read the following article.

When making important decisions it is a good idea to see things from different perspectives. Moving outside our regular way of thinking allows us to see things we might otherwise be blind to. One technique that allows you to do this was developed by a Maltese psychologist and physician, and a pioneer of lateral thinking (*i.e.,* methods of thinking concerned with changing concepts and perception), Edward de Bono. He termed it Six Thinking Hats. Each hat, or thinking strategy, allows you to see things from a different viewpoint. In the decision-making process, de Bono's technique helps you become more focused, productive, and involved. It also helps improve communication and leads to more creative thinking.

The six hats and the perspectives they represent are:

1. *White*: Facts (information known or needed)
2. *Yellow*: Optimism and a positive outlook
3. *Black*: Judgment (looking at things critically and cautiously, exploring why something may not work; spotting flaws, weak points, and risks)
4. *Red*: Feelings, hunches, gut reactions, and intuition
5. *Green*: Creativity (possibilities, alternatives, new ideas)
6. *Blue*: Control of process

And here are the hats in use:

Step 1: Present the facts of a situation (White)
Step 2: Come up with ideas on how a situation might be dealt with (Green)
Step 3: Look at the possible benefits of these ideas (Yellow)
Step 4: Look at the potential drawbacks of these ideas (Black)
Step 5: Check gut feelings about these ideas (Red)
Step 6: Take everything that was presented and make a decision (Blue)

E. Comprehension: What do each of the following colors represent in De Bono's Six Thinking Hats? Answer this question **without** looking back at the reading.

White	Yellow	Black	Red	Green	Blue

F. Rethink: Can you see the practical application of de Bono's Six Thinking Hats at work and in your personal life? Explain.

Section 4 ♦ Activity: Case studies

Directions: With a partner, read the case studies below and answer the questions that follow.

Case Study 1

Company A has a manufacturing site overseas. The host government is concerned about its hazardous[1] waste disposal[2] and air emissions[3], and wants to levy[4] heavy fines against Company A if it doesn't significantly reduce the environmental impact of its operations. Although Company A understands its corporate responsibility, reductions would hamper[5] profitability and earnings growth.

Although it seems like a Catch-22, it is up to you and your group to make a decision about the best course of action. What will you do?

[1] **hazardous**: dangerous
[2] **disposal**: process of getting rid of something
[3] **emissions**: (air) sent forth or discharged
[4] **levy**: impose (a tax)
[5] **hamper**: limit (in a negative way)

Case Study 2

Company B controls a popular World Wide Web search engine; it is a strong advocate[1] of freedom of speech and information, which has to make a decision about whether or not to enter a country that has stringent[2] censorship[3] regulations[4]. Local competition is an additional consideration.

What is the best course of action? Should the company risk pursuing its plan in the face of potential government intervention, or should the company abandon it and focus its attention elsewhere? It's an ethical dilemma that requires a sound decision on your part. What do you think should be done?

[1] **advocate**: supporter
[2] **stringent**: strict
[3] **censorship**: suppression of objectionable material
[4] **regulations**: rules

◆ Arguing ◆

Section 1 ◆ Starting Point: Arguments

A. Warm Up: Discuss the following questions with a partner.

1. Do you argue a lot?
2. When was the last time you had an argument with a friend or family member? What did you argue about?
3. When was the last time that you got into an argument at work? What happened? Was there a satisfactory outcome?

B. Group Work: Are the following sentences true (**T**), somewhat true (**S**), or not at all true (**N**) for you? Explain, referring to experiences with your family, friends, or colleagues.

When I argue . . .

1. _____ I state the problem clearly and calmly.
2. _____ I have no problem admitting that I'm wrong.
3. _____ I attempt to find common ground before focusing on differences.
4. _____ I am interested in listening to other people's opinions and I respect their position.
5. _____ I can stay focused on the problem and don't get sidetracked.
6. _____ I often get so angry that I can't think rationally.
7. _____ I often antagonize the person I am speaking to.
8. _____ I have a tendency to bring up issues that have been problematic in the past.
9. _____ I want to continue until there is nothing more to say rather than take a break to calm down and talk about it later.
10. _____ I don't like to lose.

C. As a Class: What do you think your responses to these statements say about you?

Section 2 ♦ Communication Strategies: ⊙ CD 2 track 5
Arguing and defending a point

Part 1: Read, listen to, and say these sentences and phrases.

Making a case

It's clear/obvious that _____.   Surely you can see/agree that _____.
Have you considered/thought   You have to remember that _____.
about _____?

Interrupting

Could/Can I say something?   Excuse me (for interrupting), but _____.
May I interrupt (here)?   Sorry. Can I just say _____?
I'm sorry to interrupt, but _____.   Hold on a second./Wait a minute.

Dealing with interruptions

Can/Would you let me finish, please?
Sorry, please let me finish (what I was saying).
Can I finish (what I was saying)?
Will you please stop interrupting me?

Questioning relevance

Is that (really) relevant?
That's not really relevant to _____.
What does that have to do with _____?
I think you're missing the point.

Balancing arguments

Let's look at the advantages and the disadvantages of _____.
Let's look at the pros and cons of _____.
On the one hand, _____. On the other hand, _____.

Adding related points

I'd like to add (something to) _____.
Regarding/Concerning _____.

Coming to the point of the matter

The issue is _____, not _____./ That is not the issue.
What are we really talking about (here)?
What it boils down to is _____.
It comes down to one thing _____.
It's all about _____.
In essence, _____.

Part 2: Fill in the blanks with the phrases in **bold** type. When you are finished, read
the dialogs with a partner. Then switch roles and read the dialogs again.

⊙ CD 2 track 6

That's not really relevant   Excuse me for interrupting
let's look at the pros and cons of   issue   It's pretty clear that
another topic for another day   Can you let me finish

A: _____ we should increase the gasoline tax in this
country. Doing so . . .

B: _____, but . . .

A: _____, please? As I was saying, doing so
would lower consumption, which would in turn help reduce global warming.

B: I think solar energy is the way to go.

A: _____ to what we're talking about. The
_____ is dependence on foreign oil, not alternative sources of energy.

B: But isn't that important?

A: Of course it is, but that's _____. OK?
Now, _____ raising the gasoline tax . . .

missing the point   Excuse me   interrupt
Surely you can see   What it boils down to
What do you mean exactly   Let me finish   Hold on

A: _____ that we recycle too much.

B: _____ a second! What did you say?

A: I said that we recycle too much. In fact, I think there are a lot of
misconceptions about recycling.

C: I'm sorry to _____, but . . .

A: Go ahead.

C: Misconceptions? _____?

A: I think there are a lot of myths about recycling. Take natural resources, for
example. There is a belief that we squander irreplaceable resources when we
don't recycle. But . . .

B: _____, but . . .

A: _____, please. But available stocks of most
natural resources are growing rather than shrinking. And the reason is
not recycling.

C: I recycle regularly. I think it's important.

A: I think you're _____. I'm not saying that it isn't
important. Quite the contrary. What I'm trying to say is that sometimes the
benefits are overstated. _____ is . . .

Part 3: With a partner, create and practice a dialog based on the following flow chart. Use business communication strategies from this chapter to help you. When you are finished, switch roles and create a similar dialog **without** using the flow chart.

Biotechnology is the use of living things to create useful tools and products. Genetic modification is an area of biotechnology that involves the transfer of a gene from one organism to another. One type of genetic modification that stirs a lot of public debate is genetically modified foods. One side makes the claim that genetically modified plants can help end world hunger and do away with pesticides. The other side protests that the risks are still unclear. They talk of "frankenfoods," and warn of superpests.

A1: Make a case for the benefits of genetically modified foods.

        B1: Interrupt your partner.

A2: Deal with the interruption – continue talking.

        B2: Interrupt your partner again.

A3: Deal with the interruption – allow them to speak.

        B3: State your opposition to genetically modified foods.

A4: Support your position by adding points.

        B4: Continue to support your position.

A5: Try to balance the argument.

        B5: Respond to your partner.

A6: Come to the point of the matter.

        B6: Respond to your partner.

Now make a list of 2 or 3 controversial topics. When you're finished, take different positions on each topic and practice arguing and defending a point with your partner.

Part 4: Whenever you argue about something, you need to give reasons to support your position. Use the following words to complete the sentences below.

☞ because	☞ in order to	☞ so that
☞ due to	☞ is to	☞ a reason why

1. Improved animal health is _____ you should support the development of genetically modified food.

2. The reason companies want to develop genetically modified foods _____ enhance taste and quality.

3. _____ genetically modified foods have a greater resistance to disease, pests, and herbicides, I'm in favor of this technology.

4. _____ decrease dependence on industrialized nations by developing countries, genetically modified foods should be banned.

5. The means of biotechnology must be shared _____ the world's food production isn't dominated by a few companies.

6. I am against genetically modified foods _____ the fact that the technology tampers with nature by mixing genes among species.

Part 5: Another important element of arguments is *persuasion*. Persuading is the art of getting something you want from someone who seems unwilling to provide it. People who are effective persuaders are confident, eloquent, and charming. They use logic, charisma, guilt, peer pressure, and offers of personal gain to achieve their aims. Use all of these and the tips below to persuade one of your classmates to:

1. Work overtime for you on the weekend
2. Give a presentation in front of many people on your behalf
3. Have lunch or dinner with a very annoying client
4. Transfer to another branch or subsidiary in an undesirable location
5. Take a short business trip abroad (which would entail flying a great distance twice in three days)
6. Others – think of some things relevant to your situation these days

When you are finished, switch roles and try again.

Persuasion tips

☞ Focus on the other person's interests, desires, needs, and expectation – build rapport and show that you care.

☞ Understand the situation according to their point of view.

☞ Explain how your ideas or suggestions could be the most effective techniques to implement.

☞ Demonstrate your knowledge, expertise, and experience.

☞ Show that you are reliable and trustworthy.

☞ Propose modifications or adjustments rather than complete change.

☞ Be flexible and willing to compromise.

Section 3 ♦ Reading: Debating

Debating skills are very useful in the business world. With the following exercises and article, you will learn how to use them more effectively.

A. Activate: If you could pick any one person in the world to be at your side during a business-related argument, who would it be? Why?

B. Discuss: Work with a partner and discuss the following questions.

    1. Have you ever been in a debate (*e.g.* in high school or college)?

    2. Have you ever watched a debate (*e.g.* presidential candidates)?

    3. What skills do you think someone needs in order to debate well?

C. Focus: With another pair, make a list of 3-5 current controversial or divisive business, social, or political issues, and clearly state the position of each side.

1. *Issue*:	
Pro -	Con -

2. *Issue*:	
Pro -	Con -

3. *Issue*:	
Pro -	Con -

4. *Issue*:	
Pro -	Con -

5. *Issue*:	
Pro -	Con -

What is your position? Take sides and debate **after** you have read the following article.

D. Read: Read the article below.

What is a debate? A debate is essentially an argument with rules. In a debate, two sides argue a proposition. A proposition is an issue that can be discussed from opposing points of view. A typical debate follows this order:

1. The two sides are given an issue and take positions (for or against).

2. Each side discusses their position and brainstorms support for it. *[5 minutes]*

3. The two sides make opening statements (*i.e.*, they each clearly state their position and support for it). *[1 minute]*

4. The sides openly discuss their positions, adding support and countering opposing arguments. *[10-15 minutes]*

5. Closing statements are made. *[1 minute]*

6. A winner is voted on or declared.

Although you may not follow this exact structure in the boardroom, learning how to sharpen your debating skills will help you conduct research and prepare a topic with opposing viewpoints, make a compelling presentation, and think quickly on your feet.

Here are some tips for debating well:
- ☞ Make sure you have a strong position.
- ☞ Do research and make sure that you have facts to back up what you are saying.
- ☞ Use logic to develop your case and make your points.
- ☞ Offer more than one argument that supports your point.
- ☞ Anticipate what the counterarguments are likely to be.
- ☞ Press the other side for more information, essentially asking them to prove their assertion or justify their position more clearly.
- ☞ Find flaws in reasoning and pick apart the counterarguments.
- ☞ Stick to the subject being debated.
- ☞ Be open-minded, flexible, and prepared to change your opinion.
- ☞ Be respectful and refrain from getting drawn into personal attacks.

E. Comprehension Check: Close your book and tell your partner how to debate well. If you have trouble, read through the list of tips one more time and try again.

F. Rethink: How are debating skills useful for you at work?

Section 4 ♦ Activity: Controversial issues

Directions*:* Follow the basic rules of debate as outlined in the reading, and argue some of the following topics below. You can do this in small groups or in front of the class.

- ☞ ***Friendship****:* Can men and women be just friends?
- ☞ ***Language****:* Should English be the one official world language?
- ☞ ***Society****:* Is affirmative action merely another form of discrimination?
- ☞ ***Foreign aid****:* Does foreign aid save lives and raise living standards (or create dependency)?
- ☞ ***Stem-cell research****:* Do the benefits of using human embryos outweigh the costs?
- ☞ ***Terrorism****:* Should governments negotiate with terrorists?
- ☞ ***Sports****:* Are professional athletes overpaid?
- ☞ ***Technology****:* Is the television a more significant invention than the computer?
- ☞ ***History****:* Does history really matter?
- ☞ ***Gender****:* Should same-sex marriages be legalized?

When you are finished, reflect on your performance. What did you do well? What was challenging? What do you need to work on?

♦ Negotiating ♦

Section 1 ♦ Starting Point: Are you a good negotiator?

A. Warm Up: Discuss the following questions.

1. What does "negotiate" mean?
2. How frequently do you negotiate with your family and friends? How about at work?
3. Why are negotiating skills important?

B. Group Work:

Read the following statements one by one with a partner. Decide how true each one is for you and write one of the numbers below on the line next to it. As you are working your way through the list, explain why you chose the number you did. Give examples from your life.

> "**5**" = very true
>
> "**4**" = true most of the time
>
> "**3**" = only somewhat true
>
> "**2**" = not true most of the time
>
> "**1**" = very untrue

1. ___ I am able to appreciate and be sensitive to other people's viewpoints.
2. ___ I keep promises and can be relied on.
3. ___ I am attentive to details.
4. ___ I am willing to compromise to solve any problem.
5. ___ I think and perform well under pressure.
6. ___ I am usually tactful and diplomatic.
7. ___ I am able to articulate my viewpoints clearly.
8. ___ I am a good listener.
9. ___ I enjoy researching and analyzing issues in depth.
10. ___ I am able to identify important issues quickly.

Now, add your numbers together. If your total is 45–50, you have exceptional negotiating abilities. If your total is 40–44, you are a good negotiator with a lot of potential. If your total is 35–39, you are a reasonably good negotiator, but you need to brush up on your skills. If your total is 34 or lower, you definitely need to think about your ability as a negotiator and what you can do to improve your overall effectiveness.

C. As a Class: Discuss the following questions.

1. Are you a good negotiator? Do you think your score accurately reflects your negotiating abilities?

2. Which of the following things affects your ability to negotiate successfully with someone?

   ☞ Gender

   ☞ Age

   ☞ Position in the company

   ☞ Work experience

   ☞ Educational background

   ☞ Knowledge and intelligence

   ☞ Good social skills

   ☞ Attitude

3. In order to be a better negotiator, what skills do you think you need to work on? Refer to the skills listed in Section B, Group Work.

Section 2 ♦ Communication Strategies: Negotiating

⊙ CD 2 track 7

Part 1: Read, listen to, and say these sentences and phrases.

Establishing a position

It is (absolutely) essential that ___.
It is very/extremely important that ___.
What's important (for us) is ___.
You've done a great job, but ___.
(Essentially) We're interested in ___.
(Basically) We're looking for ___.
We hope to/want to ___.
That is not a priority right now.

Making proposals

We suggest ___.
We propose ___.
We can/could offer you ___.
The best we can do is ___.

Reacting to proposals

We can go along with that.
That's acceptable.
That's a possibility. (I'll have to check with ___.)
If you ___, then we have a deal.
So, we have a deal?
We might be able to do that.
We'll have to get back to you on that.
That would be difficult.
I'm afraid we can't go along with that.
There's no way we can agree to that.

Bargaining

If you could ___, we would consider ___.
As long as ___, we can agree to ___.
Would you be interested in ___?
We realize that, but ___.
On one condition – ___.
If you can ___, we can ___.
We know that you'd prefer ___, but how about ___?
We might consider that if (you guarantee) ___.
What would you say if we offered you ___?
We would be willing to do that if (you could) ___.

Part 2: Fill in the blanks with the phrases in **bold** type. When you are finished, read the dialogs with a partner. Then switch roles and read the dialogs again.

⊙ CD 2 track 8

**We might be able to do that   What would you say if we offered you
then we have a deal   You've done a great job
I'll get back to you**

A: _____ over the past year, but we can't give you a raise right now.

B: But I've made more money for this company over the last twelve months than any other sales rep on the staff.

A: And we want to show you how much we appreciate your hard work. _____ some stock options?

B: If you give me stock options *and* more vacation time, _____.

A: _____. Let me check with management, and _____ tomorrow.

**no way we can agree   we can't go along with that
We might consider   We know that you'd prefer
It is essential that   realize**

A: _____ we agree on a realistic deadline for this project.

B: We _____ that, but there are still a few sticking points.

A: _____ to address these issues first, but how about setting a date?

B: There's _____ to that.

A: _____ an extension if you guarantee that we will move forward on this project.

B: I'm afraid _____ either.

A: Why not?

B: We're in no position to negotiate a time frame when our demands aren't being met.

**We can offer you   So we have a deal   What's important for us is
would be very difficult   On one condition
What would you say if we offered you**

A: _____ cost.

B: _____ a 12% discount if you order at least 1000 units.

A: The price is right, but it _____ for us to sell that many products.

B: _____ a 10% discount on 750 units?

A: _____ – don't charge us for delivery.

B: That's acceptable.

A: _____?

B: Yes.

Part 3: With a partner, create and practice a dialog based on the following flow chart. Use business communication strategies from this chapter to help you. When you're finished, switch roles. Create and practice a similar dialog **without** using the flow chart.

A1: Say that you would like to buy 10 refrigerators.

B1: Make a proposal – to include a sales figure ($1500 apiece).

A2: Reject the sales figure – too expensive.

B2: Bargain by lowering the sales figure ($1300).

A3: Reject the sales figure – still too expensive.

B3: Bargain some more by lowering the sales figure again ($1200), but say that is as low as you can go.

A4: React to the proposal by accepting it.

B4: Express your appreciation.

A5: State when you want the items delivered.

B5: Say that you are unable to meet that date.

A6: Request a different delivery time.

B6: Agree to the delivery time.

A7: Ask about payment terms.

B7: Say that you require a one-time payment.

A8: Say that's impossible, then ask if you can pay on an installment plan.

B8: React to this proposal and say that you will check on it.

A9: Express your appreciation.

B9: Confirm your agreement – price, delivery time, and payment plan (which you will check on).

A10: Agree and express appreciation again.

B10: Use a conversation closer.

Part 4: With the same partner, look at the list of common negotiating mistakes below. Put a ✔ next to the ones you make most often. Provide explanations as necessary.

I . . .

___ am poorly prepared.

___ dominate the discussion and don't listen enough.

___ overpower my counterpart and use tough tactics.

___ fixate on one issue, point, or position.

___ become impatient with my counterpart and rush through the agenda.

___ try to gain every advantage and deny my counterpart any benefits whatsoever.

___ trust my counterpart too much.

___ worry too much about what my counterpart thinks and feels.

___ make concessions before I have seen all of my counterpart's demands.

___ neglect to aim high enough (and settle for less than what I really want).

Can you add any other negotiating mistakes to this list, particularly ones you tend to make?

Part 5: Together with your teacher, match the negotiating tactics with their definitions. *Hint* – Look for *words* in the definition that are similar to words in the tactics (*e.g.,* **not saying anything** means "silence").

1. _b_ Use silence
    a. *check with a higher authority* before making any decisions

2. ___ Lowball
    b. sit back, wait, and let *not saying anything* work to your advantage

3. ___ Pinpoint the need
    c. use *questions* to assess your counterpart's position

4. ___ Challenge
    d. *take a break* (for a few minutes or more) to reevaluate your position

5. ___ Think things over
    e. find the *midpoint* between two offers

6. ___ Split the difference
    f. *attract* your counterpart with one offer, then *hook* them with another

7. ___ Flinch/Wince
    g. figure out what's possible after *finding out exactly* what the limits are

8. ___ Claim limited empowerment
    h. *act stunned* at the first offer (because you can always do better)

9. ___ Try test queries
    i. go for the *lowest* possible price

10. ___ Bait and switch
    j. put your counterpart on the *defensive* in order to win concessions

Now discuss the following questions.

1. Have you ever used any of these tactics when you negotiated something? If so, how well did they work?

2. Are there any tactics you haven't tried before but would like to if given the opportunity?

3. Would all of these tactics work well in your culture? Explain.

Part 6: With a partner, put yourself in the following situations and conduct negotiations. Be sure to use business communication strategies and negotiating tactics. In addition, try to avoid making any critical negotiating mistakes and strive for an outcome that is satisfactory to both of you.

1. *Negotiate the price of a house.*

A: You are a realtor. You are representing a homeowner and you are looking to make the biggest possible commission on the sale of a house for yourself. Emphasize the following points in your negotiation: good neighborhood, excellent schools, close to public transportation, spacious home, big bedrooms, old (1935) yet newly renovated (nothing needs to be repaired or replaced), big lot with a beautiful back yard, and great resale value. The asking price is $350,000.

B: You are a prospective home buyer. The property you are looking at is very attractive to you. You have questions about the following: the neighborhood, schools, public transportation, when the house was built and if it is in need of any repairs, and resale value. The absolute maximum you are willing to spend is $325,000, but you would like to buy the house for less than $300,000.

2. *Negotiate a starting salary.*

A: You have just completed your MBA degree from one of the best business schools in the world and are looking for a job as a management consultant. In addition to your prestigious degree, you worked for a management consulting firm for five years before going to graduate school. You are well qualified to work for any of the top firms around the globe. You also know that the average salary for someone in your position is approximately $100,000 per year, to include a signing bonus of about $20,000. In your job interview, you are trying to get the best possible salary and signing bonus. Emphasize that this is the job you want more than any other that you've applied for.

B: You are a prospective employer with a top management consulting firm. Every year, you recruit a select few graduates from the top business schools in the world. You are interviewing a well-qualified applicant who really wants to work for your firm, but expects to be paid well for their experience and educational background. You are prepared to offer a salary of $85,000, and a signing bonus of $15,000.

3. *Negotiate the terms of a contract.*

A: You are a wholesale shoe supplier. You offer low prices on brand-name athletic shoes to retailers, to include discounts on large orders. The most popular pair of shoes you supply is in high demand at the moment. You are willing to sell 100 pairs for $2500, 200 for $4800, and 300 for $6900.

B: You are a retail outlet owner selling athletic shoes. You would like to buy more of the hottest pair of shoes on the market from a wholesaler. You have found one wholesaler who seems to offer good deals on bulk orders. Ideally, you would like to buy 250 pairs for less than $5000.

4. *Negotiate a labor dispute.*

A: You are the owner of a professional sports team. You want to impose a salary cap* on players' salaries to keep expenditures down, as well as to balance the league so that a wealthy team cannot become dominant simply by buying all the top players. The deadline for an agreement is one week away. If a deal cannot be reached by then, the players will go on strike indefinitely. This will result in the loss of revenue and jobs at every level of the sport.

B: You are a professional athlete and a representative of the players' union. You believe that a salary cap is simply a way for the owners to get an unfair advantage in labor negotiations with players. Moreover, you strongly believe that there should be no artificial limit on what any athlete is able to earn if they have the talent.

* **salary cap** means a limit on the amount of money a team can spend on player salaries.

Section 3 ◆ Reading: Win-win negotiating

Understanding your counterpart's needs and finding a way to meet them, while meeting your needs at the same time, is what good negotiating is all about. Always strive for a win-win result in negotiations. With the following exercises and article, you will have an opportunity to examine this issue and express your opinions about it.

A. Activate: Think of two or three examples of negotiation in your personal life or at work where things went wrong and nobody was satisfied with the outcome.

B. Discuss: With a partner, share your negotiating experiences and explain what went wrong. How would each of these situations have been different if everyone involved had striven for a win-win result?

C. Focus: What do you already know about the issue of win-win negotiating? What would you like to know about this topic? Write two questions you would like the article to answer.

1

2

D. Read: Read the article.

Both parties in a negotiation want to win. A successful negotiation ends with a mutually satisfying outcome (*i.e.,* each side gets something they need). Disaster strikes when one party does not care about what the other side wants and tries to maximize its own benefit, which can lead to frustration, anger, and even revenge.

Preparation is the key to win-win results in a negotiation. There are several steps you can take to make sure that you are ready before you sit across the table from your counterpart. First of all, set clear goals and objectives. Having a clear focus about what you want to achieve will help you stay on task. If you do not know exactly what you want, you are leaving too much up to chance. This will cause unnecessary confusion and possibly derail the negotiation process.

Secondly, you need to be knowledgeable about all points and details that will be addressed in the negotiation. Being well informed will reduce anxiety and bolster your confidence. It will also show your counterpart that you are on top of your game and serious about the issues at hand.

Third, anticipate what your counterpart wants. Zero in on their beliefs, motives, and values in addition to their needs. This will help you develop your strategy and limit any surprises. It will also allow you to stay focused on your counterpart's overall aim.

Finally, make decisions about the high and low range of what you are willing to give and take. This will allow you to set clear limits and operate within those to your advantage and yet still guarantee a favorable result for your counterpart. You also need to have clear reasons why you set these limits. These should be based on thorough research about what is appropriate and desirable for both sides under the terms and conditions of what is being negotiated.

Now at the beginning of the negotiation process, state that your aim is to strive for a win-win result. Stay focused on what you want to achieve and be mindful of your counterpart's goals. If any disagreement or conflict should arise, remain calm and courteous, and seek a solution that will satisfy both sides.

While the negotiation is ongoing, ask questions to find out or verify what is important to your counterpart. Meaningfully address these and acknowledge points of agreement that you have reached periodically throughout the negotiation process. By doing this, you will refrain from focusing solely on your own needs. Remember, successful negotiation is a two-way street.

If, for whatever reason, you are unable to reach an agreement, agree to disagree for the moment. This will give you some time to think about the issues that were raised and how to go about resolving any points of contention, which you can address at the next meeting. It may take some adjustments, but a mutually agreeable outcome is certainly not out of your reach. Just let the preparation you have done and your negotiating acumen guide you to a win-win result.

E. Comprehension Check: Read the article again. When you are finished, try to fill in the following chart with details *without* looking back at the article.

Preparation – First
Preparation – Second
Preparation – Third
Preparation – Finally
Before negotiation starts
During negotiation
If unable to reach an agreement

F. Rethink:
What are the consequences of not striving for a win-win result in a negotiation?

Section 4 ♦ Activity: Negotiations and culture

Part 1: With a partner, read the text below and the points that follow.

Successful negotiation in world markets requires knowledge of historical, cultural, and religious forces that motivate and drive people in other countries. Skilled negotiators need to respect these forces, manage any differences during the negotiation, and strive for a mutually beneficial outcome. This entails working to minimize misunderstandings, building trust, and fostering positive emotions. Should negotiators choose not to do these things and operate as if they were still in their home country, conflicts will surely arise. To illustrate, take the case of Emily Johnson. She is an executive who works for a large American corporation and is about to embark on a business trip to negotiate a deal in your home country. When she arrives, she will not be very mindful of cultural differences. In fact, she will display many characteristics and beliefs that are common among business people in the United States, as well as some particular to herself. Among them:

1. She will have no problem doing business with someone she has never met before. Establishing a relationship with someone before doing business is not necessary for her.

2. After being introduced, she will use first names to address her counterparts. She believes this will make people more comfortable and relaxed.

3. She will place a high priority on time. She expects people to be punctual, and she believes that "time is money."

4. She will show herself to be action-oriented. She strongly prefers to make decisions promptly and get things done.

5. She will go after the short-term result rather than trying to foster a long-term relationship with her counterpart. She is more interested in securing the deal than fostering a lifelong partnership.

6. She will show herself to be competitive and display an individualistic attitude. Modesty, team spirit, and collectivity are less important to her than achieving personal goals.

7. She is against nepotism and bribery. She feels that both of these are unethical.

8. She speaks only English. Her presumption is that you will provide any translation assistance.

Part 2: Discuss the following questions on a point-by-point basis.

1. If Ms. Johnson conducts a business negotiation in your home country and displays these characteristics, what conflicts may arise? Why?

2. What could Ms. Johnson do to improve her negotiating skills in your country and foster a win-win relationship with business people there?

♦ Taking Responsibility ♦

Section 1 ♦ Starting Point: Responsibility

A. Warm Up: Discuss the following questions with a partner.

1. What does it mean to take responsibility for something?

2. When was the last time you had to take responsibility for something at work? What were the circumstances?

3. Have you ever let somebody else take the blame for something you did? What happened? How did the other person feel about it?

B. Group Work: What would you do? Give reasons for your answers.

As an executive in your company, you vastly underestimate the time required for your division to complete a project and you come out way over budget. Do you:

a. Accept responsibility for the error and admit to your boss and your staff that you made a mistake?

b. Say nothing (in an attempt to conceal your error) and try to correct the mistake all by yourself?

c. Attempt to deflect your responsibility for the error by spreading blame around—after all, you can't be perceived as a screw-up by your staff?

d. Other: _____

You and a colleague shared responsibility for finishing an important task by a set deadline – which you **were not** able to do. You worked very hard to get everything done on time. Your colleague, on the other hand, did not make nearly as much effort as you did. Now the two of you are being called into your director's office to explain what happened. When you go in, do you:

a. Accept responsibility as a team and not single your colleague out?

b. Remain quiet and wait for your colleague to, hopefully, step forward and admit fault?

c. Tell your director exactly what happened and blame your colleague for lack of effort?

d. Other: _____

C. As a Class: How can acting irresponsibly affect relationships at work?

Section 2 ◆ Communication Strategies: ⊙ CD 2 track 9
Accepting responsibility

Part 1: Read, listen to, and say these sentences and phrases.

Sincere apologies

    I'm so/very/really sorry.   I can't tell you how bad/terrible I feel.

Accepting the blame for something

    It's (all) my fault.   I take full responsibility.

Admitting error

My mistake.	I didn't mean to do it.
I shouldn't have said/done that.	I didn't intend to do/say that.
I (honestly) didn't mean it.	I didn't mean it that way.

Promising not to repeat a particular mistake

It won't happen again. (I promise.)
How can I make it up to you?
Is there anything I can do (to make it up to you)?
Is there any way I can make it up to you?

Forgiving

That's OK.	Don't worry about it.
It's OK.	Forget about it.

Part 2: Fill in the blanks with the phrases in **bold** type. When you are finished, read the dialogs with a partner. Then switch roles and read the dialogs again.

⊙ CD 2 track 10

fault   Do you realize   won't happen again
That's OK   completely forgot   I'm so sorry

A: Did you call the distributor and cancel the order?

B: Oh, no! I _____!

A: You're kidding! _____ how much work you've just created for us?

B: _____! It's all my _____.

A: No, I should have reminded you yesterday.

B: It _____, I promise.

A: _____. I'll get in touch with the owner and see if the boxes have already been sent.

really didn't mean to do that   What   Forget about it
Is there anything I can do   I shouldn't have said anything

A: What did you say to Susumu? He's very upset.

B: I told him that he wasn't going to get promoted.

A: _____? You had no right to say that.

B: I know _____. I'm really sorry. _____ to . . .?

A: No, there's nothing you can do.

B: I _____. It just came out.

A: _____. I'll talk to him later.

full responsibility   Please don't be mad at me
Is there any way I can make it up to you
Are you joking   don't worry about it

A: Thanks for finishing the report for me. I really appreciate it.

B: _____, but it's not done yet.

A: It's not done yet? _____? I specifically asked you if you could take care of it for me, and you said you would.

B: I know I did. I take _____.

A: It's my report. You can't take responsibility for it.

B: I'm so sorry. I just got swamped right before going home. _____ _____?

A: No. Well, _____. I'll try to finish it this morning.

Part 3: With a partner, create and practice a dialog based on the following flow charts. Use business communication strategies from this chapter to help you. When you are finished, switch roles. Create and practice a similar dialog **without** using the flow charts.

Flow chart 1

A1: Ask if your partner made copies of a report for a meeting (that starts in five minutes).

B1: Act surprised, say you forgot, and apologize.

A2: React to your partner – no time.

B2: Accept blame for the situation.

A3: Ask how you'll be able to talk about the sales figures.

B3: Admit error and apologize again.

A4: React with frustration.

B4: Promise not to repeat the same mistake again.

A5: Remain frustrated but say you'll handle it.

B5: React to your partner.

Flow chart 2

A1: Ask if your partner finished typing up an interoffice email for you.

B1: Say that you already sent it out.

A2: Act very surprised – say that you needed to make a few changes.

B2: Apologize.

A3: Say that the changes were important.

B3: Accept blame.

A4: Say that your partner should have checked with you first.

B4: Admit error and promise not to make the same mistake again.

A5: Remain surprised/upset but forgive your partner.

B5: Apologize again.

Part 4: Write a dialog based on the following roles. When you are finished, act it out in front of the class *without* your notes.

Student A:

You asked your partner to make last-minute travel arrangements for one of your company's executives last week. The executive needs to be in Geneva on a particular day to sign some contracts that will result in a lot of business for the company.

Student B:

Making the travel arrangements should have been a priority, but it slipped your mind, as you had so many things to do over the last few days. You called a number of different travel agencies this morning, but all flights are completely booked for the day your company executive needs to leave. You realize how serious this situation is. If the executive does not make it to Geneva in time, it could jeopardize the deal.

Section 3 ♦ Reading: Blame

It is easy to blame someone else for your misdeeds. But there are serious consequences of doing so. With the following exercises and article, you will have an opportunity to examine this issue and express your opinions about it.

A. Activate: Do you agree or disagree with the following quotes? Share your thoughts with a classmate.

> It's not whether you win or lose, it's how you place the **blame**.
> – *Oscar Wilde, Irish poet and novelist*

> We believe that to err is human. To **blame** it on someone else is politics.
> – *Hubert H. Humphrey, 38ᵗʰ U.S. Vice President*
> *under Lyndon Johnson (1965-69)*

> If you reveal your secrets to the wind you should not **blame** the wind for revealing them to the trees.
> – *Kahlil Gibran, Lebanese-born American philosophical essayist,*
> *novelist, and poet*

B. Discuss: Work with the same partner.

Who (*e.g.*, governments, companies, individuals) shares responsibility for . . . ?

- ☞ child labor
- ☞ conflict and war
- ☞ global warming
- ☞ illegal immigration
- ☞ infectious diseases
- ☞ overcrowding in cities
- ☞ pollution
- ☞ poor education
- ☞ poverty
- ☞ the widening gap between "haves" and "have-nots"

How do we manage these pressing global problems? Divide the problems among the class (one for each pair), then brainstorm some ideas and present them to the class. See whether your classmates agree or disagree with you and your partner.

C. Focus: Think about the last two or three things that went wrong at your organization. What happened? Who got blamed? How did it turn out? What could/should have been done differently?

D. Read: Read the article.

Do you ever blame someone else when something goes wrong at work? Shirking responsibility and looking for a scapegoat can be easy to do, especially when you consider the likely consequences of your actions. And yet blame is not without consequences of its own. It deeply affects morale, creates divisions, and results in a loss of productivity. So, instead of looking for someone else to take the fall for you, why not get to the heart of the matter and figure out what went wrong – and determine how you can prevent the same thing from happening again. Here are some helpful questions you could ask yourself toward that end:

1.   What happened?

2.   Where did things go wrong?

3.   What could we have done to prevent this from happening?

4.   How can we fix or improve the situation as it stands now? What is required?

5.   How can we ensure that this doesn't happen again?

It is not always easy to get down to brass tacks, especially when you consider that blame is an instinctive response, one that becomes potentially more defensive and self-protective as the intensity of a situation increases. However, regardless of the circumstances, it is important to take responsibility for yourself. After all, your image and self-esteem are at stake, both of which will pay huge dividends if they are seen in a positive light. So, the next time you are tempted to assign blame to someone else, just think of the costs to both you and your organization.

E. Comprehension Check: Work together and answer the following questions – **without** looking back at the article.

1. What is the main point of this article?

    _____

    _____

2. What are five questions you could ask when something goes wrong at work?

    _____

    _____

    _____

    _____

    _____

3. Why is it important to take responsibility for yourself?

    _____

    _____

F. Rethink: Answer the following questions.

1. Can you think of any famous organizations that have **shirked responsibility** and looked for a **scapegoat**?
2. Have you ever **taken the fall** for someone?
3. When something goes wrong at work, do you like to **get to the heart of the matter** and figure out went wrong, or do you usually look for a quick-fix solution and hope the problem goes away?

Section 4 ◆ Activity: Ethical dilemmas

Directions: With a partner, read the two case studies below and answer the question that follows each one.

Case Study 1

Marshall was a teenager in the late 1950s when he began smoking. By 1990, he had smoked over 20,000 packs of cigarettes and consequently succumbed to lung cancer. Before he died, he sued two cigarette manufacturers, claiming they had misinformed him and the public about the dangers of smoking and, as a result, had insidiously drawn him into a lethal nicotine habit. The Tobacco Group, one of the manufacturers targeted in the lawsuit, stated that the U.S. Congress' 1965 decision to require health warnings on cigarettes shields them from any liability.

Is The Tobacco Group liable for Marshall's death? Why or why not?

Case Study 2

In February of last year, the *Explorer*, an oil tanker of the GTN Company, accidentally struck a small atoll and spilled millions of gallons of crude oil into the waters and onto the shores of the southern part of Alaska. The damage to the beaches, wildlife, and ecology has been incalculable. The tourist industry has been devastated, and the local residents' way of life has been greatly diminished. The most minimal cleanup will cost many millions of dollars.

Upon investigation of the accident, it was discovered that the captain of the oil tanker had been drinking heavily that fateful night, and left navigation of the ship up to his first mate. The first mate had never taken charge of the ship before, and it is clear that he misread the maps, misjudged the waters, and maintained an inappropriate speed at the time of the accident. Although the impact was forceful, the oil tanker, one from an older fleet, could have survived the collision intact if the hulls had been reinforced up to current standards established six months prior to this catastrophe. This, it turns out, was an apparent oversight of the risk insurance manager. Another problem was the oil tanker's steering. The chief engineer knew that the tanker had a tendency to veer off course. The captain knew how to control the tanker in spite of this, but he warned the chief engineer of potential problems. The chief engineer routinely downplayed his warnings, saying that the captain clearly knew what he was doing. It is unclear what role the steering system played in the disaster.

Who bears the most responsibility in this situation? Why?

♦ Motivating Others ♦

Section 1 ♦ Starting Point: Motivation

A. Warm Up: Discuss the following questions with a partner.

1. What motivates you in your personal life (*e.g.,* family, health, hobbies/interests, etc.)?

2. What motivates you the most at work and in your career (*e.g.,* the company itself, colleagues, salary, benefits, advancement, *etc.*)?

B. Pair Work: Below is a list of strategies a manager can use to be supportive and help motivate employees. Put a ✔ next to each one that is true for a manager you know. Based on your answers, what do you think this manager needs to work on?

1. ☐ Helps employees solve problems.
2. ☐ Encourages employees to develop new skills.
3. ☐ Keeps informed about how employees think and feel about things.
4. ☐ Encourages employees to participate in important decisions.
5. ☐ Praises good work.
6. ☐ Encourages employees to speak up when they disagree with a decision.
7. ☐ Explains his or her actions.
8. ☐ Rewards employees for good performance.

C. As a Class: Have you ever seen any movies or TV shows, or read any books or news articles that inspired or motivated you to change your life in some way? Share some examples.

Section 2 ♦ Communication Strategies: Praising

⊙ CD 2 track 11

Part 1: Read, listen to, and say these sentences and phrases.

Praising

> Good/Nice job!
> Keep up the good work.
> Nice work on the ___.
> Impressive!
> I'm very impressed with ___.
> You did a great job!
> That was an excellent ___.
> You (definitely) have a talent for ___.

Responding to praise

> Thank you. (I appreciate it.)
> I don't deserve all the credit.
> It was a team/group effort.
> I couldn't have done it without your help.

Part 2: Fill in the blanks with the phrases in **bold** type. When you are finished, read
the dialogs with a partner. Then switch roles and read the dialogs again.

⊙ CD 2 track 12

Keep up the good work   impressed
seal the deal   can assure you

A: I was very _____ with the way you handled
    yourself at the meeting.
B: Really? I was so nervous!
A: I _____, nobody could tell.
B: That's a relief. I know how important the clients were.
A: You helped _____. There's no doubt about that.
B: Thanks.
A: _____!

team effort   I appreciate that   great job
you have a real talent for   clutch
I don't deserve all the credit

A: I think you did a _____ on your presentation yesterday.
B: Thanks, but _____.
A: But you really came through in the _____.
B: Believe me, I had a lot of help. It was definitely a _____.
A: Nonetheless, _____ public speaking.
B: Thank you. _____.

Part 3: With a partner, create and practice a dialog based on the following flow chart. Use business communication strategies from this chapter to help you. When you are finished, switch roles. Create and practice another version of the same dialog.

A1: Praise your partner for something they did well.

           B1: Respond to praise – group effort.

A2: Reiterate how impressed you were.

           B2: Respond to praise – don't deserve all credit.

A3: Single your partner out (from the rest of the group).

           B3: Respond to praise.

A4: End conversation with more praise.

Part 4: Do a role play to act out the following situations.

    ☞   Commend someone for solving a difficult problem for you.

    ☞   Praise the performance of someone in a difficult situation.

    ☞   Celebrate the success of a team whose hard work paid off.

Part 5: Make a list of the different ways (not expressions) in which you could let someone know that they are doing a great job.

Example: Send an email, to include a Cc (a "carbon copy") to your boss.

Part 6: Think of someone you work with who definitely deserves some praise. Answer the following questions about them. Then share your answers with the class.

1. What do they add to your organization?

2. How have they improved lately?

3. Why are you glad they are an employee at your company?

4. What would you miss if they were to leave?

Section 3 ◆ Reading: Hierarchy of needs

Every person has basic physiological and psychological needs in life that need to be met. Satisfying them is critical to our survival. With the following exercises and article, you will have an opportunity to examine this issue and express your opinions about it.

A. Activate: What are your basic needs in life? Make a list.

B. Discuss: Compare your list with a partner. What is similar? What is different? Are there additional needs that you would like to add to your list?

C. Focus: Make a master list of needs (from your class) on the board or a piece of paper. Try to put the needs in groups or categories.

D. Read: Read the following article.

In 1943, American psychologist Abraham Maslow wrote a paper titled "A Theory of Human Motivation." The theory he proposes is that human beings seek to satisfy a hierarchy of human needs. He groups these needs into five categories: physiological, safety, love, esteem, and self-actualization. These categories are usually depicted as a pyramid like the one below.

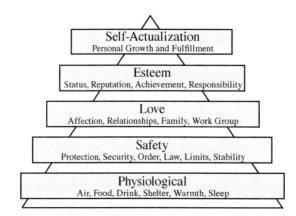

Maslow calls the four lower levels deficiency needs, and the top level growth needs. The deficiency needs must be met to ensure our survival. The growth needs, on the other hand, are psychological. They help shape and mold our behavior. According to Maslow, as needs on the lower part of the pyramid are met, we strive to satisfy higher levels of needs, with growth forces propelling us upward.

In a reaction to Maslow's hierarchy, Yale psychology professor Clayton P. Aldefer proposed a similar theory of human motivation termed ERG Theory in 1969. ERG Theory distinguishes three categories of human needs that influence workers' behavior – existence (Maslow's first two levels), relatedness (Maslow's third and fourth levels), and growth (Maslow's fourth and fifth levels). Alderfer's theory states that the order of importance for these three categories varies for each individual. He believes that human beings do not follow a predetermined hierarchy to satisfy higher levels of needs. Sometimes relatedness is more important than existence or growth, and we seek to satisfy this need without having to fulfill the other two. And sometimes we try to satisfy more than one need, or all of them simultaneously. If, for some reason, a higher-level need is not fulfilled, we may regress to a lower-level need that seems easier to satisfy. Alderfer called this the frustration-regression principle.

Regardless of their differences, both theories assume that all human activity is motivated by needs. And many studies of job satisfaction have shown that the strongest correlate of satisfaction is motivation. The people who express the greatest satisfaction with their work are those who demonstrate the strongest motivation.

E. Comprehension Check: Without looking back at the article, fill in the following boxes with examples of each type of need.

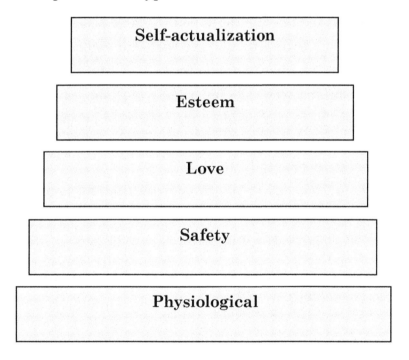

Now answer the following questions.

1. How are Maslow's and Alderfer's theories of motivation different from one another?

2. Which of the two theories makes more sense to you? Why?

F. Rethink: Which needs of Maslow's hierarchy are not being met for you at work (or because of work)? What do you require for increased job satisfaction?

Section 4 ♦ Activity: How motivated are you?

Directions*:* Work with a partner. Put a ✔ next to each statement that is true
for you. Discuss any points of interest by giving examples from your personal
or professional life.

1. ☐ It is your destiny to accomplish many great things.
2. ☐ You can move yourself to take productive action anytime and anyplace.
3. ☐ When you say you're going to do something, you do it.
4. ☐ No matter what your goal is, you always find a way to achieve it.
5. ☐ You have an unquenchable thirst for knowledge.
6. ☐ You love getting important things done.
7. ☐ You see opportunity all around you.
8. ☐ When you begin any new tasks or project, you constantly imagine succeeding.
9. ☐ You always give your best effort in everything you do.
10. ☐ You focus on activities that reflect the positive purpose of your life.
11. ☐ Most experiences in your life teach you valuable lessons.
12. ☐ You are driven by the desire to be the best that you can be.
13. ☐ You have a never-say-die spirit; you finish everything you start.
14. ☐ You are a big thinker: you take big actions and you get big results.
15. ☐ You connect best with successful, purpose-driven people.
16. ☐ To you there is nothing more exciting than winning.
17. ☐ You inspire other people to be their best.
18. ☐ With your quiet, clear mind, you can stay focused for long periods of time.
19. ☐ A big reason for your success is your close attention to small details.
20. ☐ Like an artist, you are making every day a great masterpiece.

What do you think your responses to these statements say about your motivation
in life, both at home and at work?

◆ Holding Meetings ◆

Section 1 ◆ Starting Point: Meetings

A. Warm Up: Discuss the following questions with a partner.

1. Do you enjoy meetings? Why or why not?
2. How much of your day do you spend in meetings?
3. Which of the following types of meetings do you participate in most often?

☞ Ad-hoc   ☞ Headquarters   ☞ Planning

☞ Brainstorming   ☞ Information   ☞ Project

☞ Customer/Client   ☞ Management   ☞ Status

☞ Decision making   ☞ Off-site (workshop)   ☞ Team/Staff

☞ Emergency   ☞ One-to-one   ☞ Other(s): _____

4. What is a typical meeting like where you work?
5. What makes a good meeting?

B. Group Work 1: Compare the following characteristics of effective meetings to those of the ones you regularly attend. Put a ✔ next to the characteristics that are typical for the meetings at your office.

1. ☐ An agenda is prepared prior to the meeting and given to the participants.
2. ☐ Only the people who are needed are invited to attend.
3. ☐ The facilities are adequate and comfortable.
4. ☐ Equipment is readily available and works properly.
5. ☐ The meeting begins on time.
6. ☐ A clear goal or purpose for the meeting is stated.
7. ☐ The agenda is closely followed.
8. ☐ Time is managed efficiently.
9. ☐ Minutes of the meeting are taken and sent to participants after it is over.
10. ☐ The meeting leader follows up with participants on action agreed to during the meeting.

How can meetings at your office be improved?

C. Group Work 2: Below is a list of common problems people have with meetings. Put an **X** next to the three that bother you the most, and explain why.

☞ ___ People who arrive late

☞ ___ Too many interruptions

☞ ___ People who always think they are right

☞ ___ Length – too long

☞ ___ Distracting side conversations

☞ ___ People who talk too much

☞ ___ People who bring up unrelated matters

☞ ___ People who come unprepared

☞ ___ People who are unclear or vague

☞ ___ Not useful or informative (waste of time)

Can you think of any other annoying problems at meetings?

Section 2 ◆ Communication Strategies:
Holding a meeting

Part 1: Read, listen to, and say these sentences and phrases.

Starting

> Is everybody ready?   Let's get started.

Introducing the agenda

> Does everybody have a copy of the agenda?
> Have you all received a copy of the agenda?

Stating the purpose

> The purpose/objective/aim of this meeting is ___.
> We're here today to ___.

Setting the agenda

> There are three items on the agenda: ___.
> We've got several items on the agenda.

Opening the first item

> Let's start with ___./Let's begin by ___.
> The first item on the agenda is ___.

Moving on to the next item

> The next item on the agenda is ___.
> Does anybody have anything else to add?
> Are we ready to move on?
> Let's move on to the next item.

Postponing

> Let's skip the next item.
> Let's save that for another meeting/time.

Referring forward and back

> We'll get to that (a little) later.
> We'll come to that in a minute.
> As I said earlier ___.
> We talked about that earlier.

Summarizing

So, to sum up, ____.
To summarize, ____.
To summarize what we've been talking about, ____.
To be clear, we've decided/agreed to ____.

Closing

I think that just about covers it/everything.
Is there anything more to discuss/talk about?
Let's stop there.
I believe we're done (for today).

Part 2: Work in groups of four. Fill in the blanks with the phrases below. When you are finished, read the dialogs with your partners. Then switch roles and read the dialogs again. Repeat as necessary.

⊙ CD 2 track 14

**save that for another meeting   Let's begin by   agenda
We'll get to that later   out of time   our objective today is to
brainstorming   Let's stop there   Let's move on to the next item**

A: Does everyone have a copy of the _____?
All: Yes.
A: As you can see, _____ identify ways to help bring this company back to profitability. This is going to require a bit of _____. _____ figuring out a way to boost sales. Anyone?
B: We could send our customers free sample products when they order something from the catalog.
A: Good idea! Let me write that down. Any others? . . .
A: [*Later*] _____ – cutting costs. Any ideas?
C: We could cross-train employees instead of calling in temporary help, which is what we usually do.
A: Cross-train employees . . . Good. Others?
D: How about sending an email newsletter instead of a printed newsletter?
B: Oh, that reminds me. We should upgrade our computers.
A: _____. For now, just focus on cutting costs. . .
A: [*Later*] Right. The third item on the agenda . . . No, let's _____ _____. OK, the last thing we need to talk about is salaries. I'm afraid we can't afford to give anybody a raise this year.
C: But that's not fair.
A: As I said earlier, it's all about helping this company get out of the red.
C: I realize that, but . . .
A: Actually, this is more of an announcement rather than a topic of discussion. Please understand our situation. All right, it looks like we're just about _____. _____ for today.

Part 3: Work in a group of three. Create and practice a dialog based on the following flow chart. Use business communication strategies from this chapter to help you. When you are finished, switch roles. Create and practice the same dialog. Repeat as necessary.

Situation: You own and operate a travel agency in a suburban neighborhood. You have just learned that your main competitor will open a competing travel agency across the street within three months. You need to have a meeting to discuss the impact this will have on your business. You have sent the agenda to the two employees you will be meeting with.

1. A: Start the meeting and introduce the agenda.

    B: Respond to A.
    C: Respond to A.

2. A: Explain the situation, set the agenda (impact on business), and ask for initial reaction to situation.

    B: Respond to A (surprised and concerned).
    C: Respond to A and B (surprised and concerned).

3. A: Open first item (ask about impact on business).

    C: Respond to A.
    B: Respond to A and C.

4. A: Respond to B and C, then move on to the next item (how to retain customers).

    C: Respond to A.
    B: Respond to A and C.

5. A: Respond to B and C, postpone the next item, and then move on to the next item (increase sales).

    B: Ask about construction plans for the new agency.

6. A: Refer forward (another meeting) and ask B to stay focused on current item.

    B: Respond to A.
    C: Respond to B.

7. A: Respond to B and C, then ask for further input on the three items discussed at the meeting.

    C: Respond to A.
    B: Respond to A and C.

8. A: Respond to B and C, then close the meeting (being sure to say that more discussion on this situation is needed).

Part 4: Brainstorming is a great way to generate a lot of ideas at a meeting. In the same group, take five minutes to come up with and write down as many ideas as you can about each of the topics below.

Topic 1: What are some of the best ways to invest your money?

Topic 2: How can companies attract a lot of attention when they launch a new product?

Topic 3: As the key to a successful business is maintaining a steady customer base, how do you build customer loyalty?

To promote creativity during this process, use some of the phrases on the left. Conversely, avoid using the phrases on the right. These are idea killers.

Phrases to use:	*Phrases to avoid*:
Good/Nice!	That's ridiculous/absurd/crazy.
Great/Excellent idea!	We tried that before. (It didn't work.)
I like that!	That'll never work.
We can do a lot with that (idea).	That's not practical.
That'll work.	Let's get back to reality.
I'm glad you brought that up.	It's (totally/completely) unrealistic.
I never thought of that.	It's impossible.
We're doing well.	There's no way it can be done.
We're on a roll!	No way!
Keep the (good) ideas coming!	You're absolutely wrong.

When you are finished, share your ideas with the class. Make a master list on the board or another piece of paper. Then decide which ideas are the strongest for each topic. If you need to be critical of certain items on the list, soften your language by using the word "but" (*e.g.,* "That's a good idea, *but . . .*").

Part 5: Match the method of stimulating discussion during meetings on the left with its corresponding question or statement on the right. Follow the example.

1. _f_ Ask for feelings and opinions

    a. It's still not clear to me. What do I do when ____?

2. ____ Paraphrase

    b. What are some other ways to approach this problem?

3. ____ Ask for a summary

    c. How do you think we should proceed on this?

4. ____ Ask for clarification

    d. Is this the best way to achieve our objectives?

5. ____ Ask for examples

    e. Let's see a show of hands. Who's in favor of this proposal?

6. ____ Explore in more detail

    f. What do you think about this?

7. ____ Initiate action

    g. Can you give us some examples?

8. ____ Do a quick survey

    h. If we do it this way, what's the worst thing that could happen next year?

9. ____ Check goals

    i. Let me restate your last point to see if I understand.

10. ____ Look into the future

    j. I think we need to summarize what we've been talking about.

Part 6: Can you think of any useful phrases for the following functions in managing meetings? Work in groups first. Then check with your teacher.

1. Asking for reactions (to something that was said during the meeting)

2. Dealing with interruptions (from other people)

3. Sticking to the point (to make sure what is said is relevant to the meeting)

4. Slowing down (to examine something closely or in more detail)

5. Establishing consensus (to see if everyone agrees about something)

Section 3 ♦ Reading: Effective meetings

When you consider that roughly one-third of our time at work is spent in meetings, it is essential to use it productively. With the following exercises and article, you will have an opportunity to examine this issue and express your opinions about it.

A. Activate: Work with a partner.

Part 1: Put the following steps of a typical agenda in order from 1 to 8.

☞ ____ Establish the follow-up procedures.
☞ ____ Bring up the problem to be discussed.
☞ ____ Assign tasks to carry out the plan.
☞ ____ Begin the meeting with an opening statement.
☞ ____ Decide among possible solutions.
☞ ____ Bring the meeting to a close (see Part 2 below).
☞ ____ Develop a plan to solve the problem.
☞ ____ Brainstorm solutions to the problem.

Part 2: Now put the following closing remarks of a meeting in order.

☞ ____ Set a date and time for a new meeting, *etc.*
☞ ____ Make sure that no one has anything else to say.
☞ ____ Ask if all participants understand and are satisfied with your summary.
☞ ____ Indicate that it is time to bring the meeting to a close.
☞ ____ Summarize the main points of the meeting.
☞ ____ Thank the participants for coming.
☞ ____ Restate the purpose of the meeting.

B. Read: Work with a partner. Read the following article.

Meetings are an important vehicle for communication and an integral part of most people's jobs. Many of the meetings we attend, however, could be run much more efficiently. One way to be more productive is to ask yourself the following questions before and after you lead your next meeting:

Is a meeting really necessary?

A meeting can be avoided if the same information can be covered and documented in an email, a memo, a brief report, or a public folder on your company's network. Only have a meeting if two-way information sharing is required.

Who needs to attend?

Only have people come if they are going to contribute to and/or get something out of the meeting.

What's the agenda?

Make sure you are clear about what you want to talk about and accomplish.

Does everyone have a copy of the agenda before the meeting starts?

Provide each participant with a brief description of the meeting's objectives, a list of the topics to be covered, and any necessary background information a few days in advance. This will go a long way to ensure that your meeting goes smoothly and stays on track.

Did I document and follow up on meeting decisions and task assignments?

You should take notes or minutes (or assign someone to do so). Minutes of a meeting are just written documentation needed for reference to be sure you do not have to make the same decision again at a later date, and to communicate meeting results to others. Minutes are also a tool to follow up on task assignments that have been accepted by participants. The minutes should indicate who will do what, and by when.

How did it go?

Addressing what went well and what needs work at the end of each meeting will help improve the next one. It is also a great way to polish your facilitation skills.

C. Comprehension: What are six questions you could ask to make meetings more productive? Answer this question **without** looking back at the article.

1. _____

2. _____

3. _____

4. _____

5. _____

6. _____

D. Rethink: Do you think you are (or would be) a good meeting leader? Why or why not?

Section 4 ♦ Activity: Leading meetings

Directions: Work in groups of three. Use the following topics and practice leading decision-making meetings. Be sure to follow the agenda and end with some closing remarks.

Situation 1:

> You work for an entertainment company. Your company is losing millions of dollars every year because of counterfeit DVDs and illegal downloading. You need to brainstorm a list of ways to deal with this serious problem (agenda item 1), identify which of these ways would be most feasible (agenda item 2), and draw up a timetable to put your plan into action (agenda item 3).

Situation 2:

> You and your colleagues have been asked to give a presentation on preventing sexual harassment in the workplace. You need to brainstorm a list of ways to do this (agenda item 1), choose the three most important ones (agenda item 2), and organize your presentation (agenda item 3).

Situation 3:

> You and your colleagues work for your national government, which is growing increasingly concerned about the widening income gap in your country. You need to discuss the problems caused by the income gap (agenda item 1), identify actions the government could take to redress the inequity (agenda item 2), and anticipate what the public reaction to these might be (agenda item 3).

◆ Handling Criticism ◆

Section 1 ◆ Starting Point: Criticism

A. Warm Up: Discuss the following questions with a partner.

    1. How often do you criticize yourself? How about members of your family? Friends?

    2. How critical are you of the company you work for and your colleagues?

    3. Do you tend to keep criticism to yourself or do you usually vocalize it?

    4. When you do give criticism, is it constructive or more like a complaint?

B. Group Work: Make a list of times when you or someone you know got in trouble at work and was reprimanded as a result. Add to the examples below.

Arrived to work late more than once
Did a bad job on a task or assignment

Now make a master list on the board. Add examples from other groups into the box above. You will use these later in this unit.

C. As a Class: What is the best way to handle criticism? Write any answers you or your classmates come up with in the box below.

Section 2 ♦ Communication Strategies: Handling criticism

⊙ CD track 15

Part 1: Read, listen to, and say these sentences and phrases.

Acknowledging

You're (absolutely) right.
I see/understand what you're saying.
I should have known better.

Asking for specification

Can you be more specific/exact?
Can you give me an example?
What exactly do you want (me to do)?
What did I do that makes you think that?

Explaining

I can explain.
Let me explain.
If you'll allow to me to explain, ___.
If you give me a chance to explain, ___.

Expressing thanks

I appreciate your telling me that.
Thanks for pointing that out (to me).
Thanks for letting me know.
Thanks for bringing that to my attention.

Part 2: Fill in the blanks with the phrases in **bold** type. When you are finished, read the dialogs with a partner. Then switch roles and read the dialogs again.

⊙ CD 2 track 16

Thanks for letting me know   **Let me explain**

What did I do that makes you think that

A: I need to speak with you in my office. You seem to be having trouble getting things done on time lately.

B: _____?

A: You didn't submit your report by 5:00 yesterday as I asked you to. You also should've consolidated the sales figures by now.

B: _____. I'm really stressed out with all the extra work lately.

A: We all are. You're just going to have to come in early or stay late like everyone else. Do whatever it takes to meet your deadlines.

B: I'm sorry, it won't happen again. _____.

You're absolutely right   **more specific**

you'll allow me to explain   **bringing that to my attention**

Can you give me an example   **understand what you're saying**

A: I'd like to see you in my office. There have been a few complaints about you recently.

B: Really? Can you be _____?

A: Basically, customers think that you're being rude to them.

B: Rude? _____?

A: One customer said that you snapped at her when she asked you for help.

B: Oh, I remember her. If _____ . . .

A: You just can't do that.

B: I _____. But she just kept asking me question after question. There were other customers in the store.

A: I realize dealing with difficult people isn't easy, but that's part of your job.

B: _____. Thanks for _____

_____.

Part 3: With a partner, create and practice a dialog based on the following flow charts. Use business communication strategies from this chapter to help you. When you are finished, switch roles. Create and practice a similar dialog **without** using the flow charts.

Flow chart 1

A1: Ask to speak to your partner in your office.

B1: Respond to your partner.

A2: State problem – late three times this week.

B2: Offer an explanation.

A3: Respond to your partner (emphasize the need to be punctual).

B3: Acknowledge your partner.

A4: Respond to your partner.

B4: Express thanks.

Flow chart 2

A1: Ask to speak to your partner in your office.

B1: Respond to your partner.

A2: State problem – several mistakes at work recently.

B2: Ask for specification.

A3: Bring up most recent problem – delivering the wrong order to an important customer.

B3: Offer an explanation.

A4: Don't accept the explanation.

B4: Acknowledge your partner and apologize.

A5: Reprimand your partner.

B5: Respond to your partner and express thanks.

Part 4: Below is a list of strategies to handle criticism. Decide which ones are effective and which ones are not. Reword the ineffective ones to make them effective. Follow the example.

1. Do not pay attention to what is being said. → Pay attention to what is being said.

2. Explain your rationale.

3. Respond defensively and argue.

4. Pretend to understand if you are uncertain about what is being said.

5. Do not be silent.

6. Hold a grudge.

7. Do not get caught up in negative thoughts and insecurities.

8. Take it personally.

9. Ask questions to clarify.

10. Reach agreement on how you will change.

When you are finished, discuss why each one is important. Draw on personal experience. Think of times when you did the opposite of what is suggested above and what happened as a result.

Part 5: Practice handling criticism. Select one situation from Group Work in Starting Point (page 165) and write a dialog with one of your classmates. Be sure to incorporate the strategies from the previous section. When you are finished, perform your dialog in front of the class without using your notes. When you are listening to your classmates, think about how well each of them handled criticism (*i.e.*, what they did well or what they need to work on) and offer any helpful suggestions that you can.

Section 3 ♦ Reading: Constructive criticism

Criticizing someone you work with is never easy. However, it is possible to turn negative feedback into something positive and productive. With the following exercises and article, you will have an opportunity to examine this issue and express your opinions about it.

A. Activate: When was the last time you had to criticize someone at work? What was the situation? What needed to be done? How did you handle it?

B. Discuss: How can you transform a potentially negative, relationship-damaging encounter with a colleague (*e.g.* an argument over something that happened at work) into a motivating and beneficial experience for both of you?

C. Focus: What would you do in the following situation? Think about your answer to the previous question

You asked one of your employees to attend some conference workshops, take detailed notes of the proceedings at each one, and write a report of his findings. When you get the report, it is clear that he did not do what you asked. In fact, you wonder if he spent any time at the conference at all. Moreover, the report looks as if it was sloppily put together the night before. You are frustrated because the information from the conference workshop would have been very useful to make an important business decision, and you are disappointed in the lack of professionalism of someone you counted on and trusted.

D. Read: Work with a partner. Read the following article.

Criticizing someone you work with is never an easy thing to do. However, if you are tactful and professional, not only will you minimize any undue friction in the office, you will also earn the respect of the people you work with and get a greater degree of productivity from them. The following tips will help you be more constructive the next time you are put in this position:

Know the facts. Be sure you have all pertinent information before confronting someone. Not doing so could undermine your efforts, as well as potentially cost you some credibility around the office.

Consider the place and time. Criticizing someone in front of other people is never a good idea, nor is bringing up a difficult subject when someone is too exhausted to deal with it.

Begin and end with praise. Starting with a compliment at the beginning of the conversation will make it easier for your suggestions to be accepted. Ending with something positive will indicate that you are not upset or angry.

Show empathy. Imagine yourself in the shoes of the person you are criticizing. Try to understand their vulnerability and be aware of how they are bracing themselves for what you are about to say.

Monitor your language. Be careful about phrasing and the tone of your voice. What you say, and how you say it, will go a long way to getting your message across.

Make use of humor. A good laugh and a bit of levity will ease the pressure and help the person you are criticizing be more open to what you have to say.

Address the behavior not the person. Focus on suggestions for improvement, being careful not to insult someone in the process. In other words, separate the person from their work as much as you can.

Provide opportunities for response. Allowing someone a chance to explain themselves, both during the conversation and at the end, will help make them feel better about the situation to some degree.

Refrain from repetition. With criticism, once is enough. Repeated suggestions will only result in heightened levels of stress and frustration.

Improve the situation together. Providing direct support will assure that positive and productive adjustments are made soon.

C. Comprehension Check: List 10 things to keep in mind when trying to give constructive criticism, *without* looking back at the article. Use the following prompts to help you.

1. Know . . .
2. Consider . . .
3. Begin . . .
4. Show . . .
5. Monitor . . .
6. Make . . .
7. Address . . .
8. Provide . . .
9. Refrain . . .
10. Improve . . .

F. Rethink: Do you think most of the criticism you receive is constructive? If not, why do you think people are so undiplomatic, direct, or insulting?

Section 4 ◆ Activity: What went wrong?

Directions:

What went wrong in the following situations? How could each person have responded differently? How would the outcome have been different? What should be done now to reconcile any differences? Think about what you learned in this unit.

Situation 1:

Junko argued with Rafael over who was at fault for failing to close an important business deal. Although both people share responsibility, Junko blamed Rafael for this serious setback. The two of them aren't on speaking terms now.

Situation 2:

Nicholas was harshly criticized for his performance on a task. When facing his boss, he remained silent and offered no rationale to explain what went wrong. Later, because of this situation, he became increasingly insecure about his ability to do his job well, and eventually quit.

Situation 3:

Ming was reprimanded by Diego, one of his colleagues, over something he deemed trivial. He took it personally and held a grudge against him. Not being able to forgive and forget, Ming's attitude towards Diego continues to negatively affect their relationship in the office.

Situation 4:

Thea was focused on a personal problem when she was being reprimanded by her boss. She pretended to understand what her boss was saying at the time, but, in actuality, she was not paying attention at all and forgot everything her boss told her. Now Thea is being called into her boss's office and is about to be scolded for the exact same thing.

Situation 5:

Henri humiliated one of his co-workers at a staff meeting. He criticized his co-worker's weak presentation skills in a personally demeaning manner, belittling his co-worker by comparing his co-worker's performance to that of other people on staff who have superior public speaking abilities. Henri's co-worker is now ashamed to show his face at the office, let alone deal with Henri in any productive way.

Situation 6:

> Nhu was severely reprimanded for negligence in legal proceedings right before an important meeting with her company's board of directors. Her anxiety about the meeting was replaced by fears of getting fired, causing her to lose focus on the task at hand.

Situation 7:

> Carlos repeatedly criticized his colleague about an error in judgment during negotiations with a supplier. His colleague, a new employee with the company, was not sure what he was doing when the mishap occurred. Rather than offer helpful advice or constructive feedback, Carlos simply berated his colleague for his poor performance. The two of them will be in a similar situation next week. Needless to say, Carlos' colleague is very worried and unsure of himself heading into the next negotiation.

Situation 8:

> In the space below, come up with your own situation and pose it to your classmates. Ask them what went wrong and how things might have turned out differently if one or more of the people involved had spoken or behaved in a different way.

♦ Managing Stress ♦

Section 1 ♦ Starting Point: Workplace stress

A. Warm Up: Discuss the following questions with a partner.

1. Do you get stressed out easily?
2. Do you work well under pressure?
3. What causes you the most stress at work these days?
4. What causes you stress away from the office?
5. What has been the single most stressful thing in your life so far?

B. Group Work: What problems can workplace stress cause for a company? Make a list in the box below.

> a fall in productivity
> poor decision-making

C. As a Class: Think of some ways to relieve stress. What have you done that works well for you?

Section 2 ♦ Communication Strategies: ⊙ CD 2 track 17
Managing stress

Part 1: Read, listen to, and say these sentences and phrases.

Offering advice

You should/shouldn't ____.

If I were you/in your position, I'd ____.

(I think) You'd better ____.

I think you should ____.

Why don't you ____?

How about ____?

It might/would be a good idea if you ____.

You'll have to ____.

You're going to have to ____.

You could also/always ____.

Have you thought about ____?

Whatever you do, don't ____.

Try ____ for a while.

I suggest/recommend ____.

One thing you could do is ____.

I always find ____ helpful (when ____).

You might want to try ____.

This works pretty well: ____.

Asking for advice

Should I ____?

How should I ____?

Do you think I should ____?

What do you think I should ____?

Do you have any ideas about how to ____?

If you were me/in my situation, what would you do?

Can you give me some advice?

Are you suggesting ____?

Do you have any suggestions/recommendations?

Can you recommend ____?

Part 2: Fill in the blanks with the phrases in **bold** type. When you are finished, read
the dialogs with a partner. Then switch roles and read the dialogs again.

⊙ CD 2 track 18, first part

Why don't you   Whatever you do   You could also
If you were in my situation, what would you do

A: I feel that people at work don't appreciate the job I do. _____
_____?

B: _____ talk to your boss about it? You might be
surprised by what she has to say. _____ check in
with your colleagues. I bet they count on you more than you realize. Maybe
everyone's just caught up in all the work they have to do. _____
_____, don't make a big deal of it. You don't want to come across
in the wrong way.

I also recommend   It might be a good idea
You might also try getting

A: Business is great, but I'm at the office seven days a week now – and I'm
bringing work home every night. I'm so exhausted.

B: _____ to join a gym. Working out is always a
big help for me. _____ in to work a
little earlier, and try to be a little more efficient when you're there. Make it your
goal to leave work at the office. That's key for me. _____
power napping. A 15 to 20 minute snooze always gives me a boost in the
afternoon.

I always find   If you have a chance
Do you have any ideas about   One other thing you could do

A: I'm being transferred to our branch in Istanbul. _____
_____ dealing with such a big change?

B: _____, I think you should head over there for a
visit before you start working. Getting the lay of the land will help a lot.
_____ is meet with your new boss.
Getting to know him will help ease the transition. _____
that talking to other people who've been in a similar situation is helpful, too.
See if anyone on the staff has made a similar move in recent months.

Part 3: Put a ✔ next to the items that have caused you stress at work.

1. ☐ Long working hours
2. ☐ Increased workload
3. ☐ Interruptions (*e.g.,* telephone calls, walk-in visits, supervisor's demands)
4. ☐ Deadlines
5. ☐ Unreasonable performance demands
6. ☐ No feedback (unsure how you're doing)
7. ☐ Feeling undervalued or unappreciated
8. ☐ No room for advancement
9. ☐ Tedious, monotonous, or meaningless tasks
10. ☐ Lack of control over work
11. ☐ Poor communication

   (*e.g.,* lack of information, misunderstanding, misinterpretation)

12. ☐ Unclear policies
13. ☐ Interpersonal conflict with colleagues
14. ☐ Difficult boss
15. ☐ Workplace change – place, position, and/or duties
16. ☐ Bullying or harassment
17. ☐ Fear of making mistakes or doing something wrong
18. ☐ Poor physical working environment (*e.g.,* temperature, noise, lack of privacy)
19. ☐ Office politics
20. ☐ Commute to the office

Other(s):_____

_____

With a partner, discuss why each item you checked or added has been stressful for you.

Part 4: Practice asking for and offering advice. Use role play to act out some of the situations in Part 2. Follow the examples in Part 1. Switch roles after each one. Repeat as necessary.

Section 3 ◆ Reading: Stress management tips

Job stress is a chronic condition caused by factors in the workplace that negatively affect our performance and our overall physical and psychological well-being. Finding ways to alleviate and manage stress is crucial if we want to stay on top of things.

A. Activate: Work with a partner. Match each of the three stages of stress on the left with its definition on the right.

1. ___ Alarm Stage   a. Adaptive efforts by the body to cope with or resolve stress and return to a normal state of being

2. ___ Resistance Stage   b. Fatigue sets in, ability to concentrate or stay on task decreases, body begins to malfunction, and there is an increased susceptibility to illness

3. ___ Exhaustion Stage   c. Rush of energy and pressure; body starts preparing for fight or flight

B. Discuss: Talk about times when you felt any of the following stress signals as a result of situations at work. What was going on at the time?

* Low job satisfaction
* Physical illness (fatigue, headache, nausea)
* Sleep disturbances
* Anxiety and restlessness
* Feeling overwhelmed
* Irritation, frustration, anger, or resentment
* Moodiness
* Repetitive or racing thoughts
* Depression
* Desire to escape or run away
* Apathy
* Chronic fatigue
* Low energy and stamina
* Lack of confidence
* Inability to concentrate
* Memory loss
* Poor judgment
* Increased alcohol or drug use

C. Focus: Do you ever use any of the following techniques to alleviate or manage stress?

✶ Stretch and exercise	✶ Take a mental vacation
✶ Breathe deeply	✶ Drink plenty of water
✶ Meditate	✶ Care for a pet
✶ Do yoga	✶ Take a hot shower or bath
✶ Practice tai chi	✶ Enjoy the outdoors
✶ Use aromatherapy	✶ Listen to music
✶ Get a massage	✶ Practice mindfulness
✶ Take regular breaks	✶ Keep a journal
✶ Power nap	✶ Sit and think

Which ones do you think would be useful for you? Why?

D. Read: Read the following article.

Are you feeling stressed around the clock? If so, you're not alone.

When the workday finally comes to an end, most people look forward to heading home or going out with friends and unwinding. But for many, it is difficult to shake the anxiety of the office. They carry the stress with them and let it affect their personal lives negatively, which ends up exacerbating the pressure they already have.

Here are some tips on how to leave stress at work:

☞   ***Try to end the day in the most relaxing way possible.*** Take care of the more demanding tasks as soon as you are able to, saving the easier jobs you have for the last hour before you go home.

☞   ***Get organized.*** Plan for the day ahead by making a list of what needs to be done and how you plan to complete each task. This should help minimize any overnight unrest.

☞   ***Maintain perspective.*** Your troubles are temporary, no matter how serious they are or how much you worry about them. They will pass and will likely be of little importance in the future.

☞   ***Connect with others.*** Talking with someone else can help clear your mind of confusion so that you can focus on problem solving.

☞ *Use your commute to separate work from the rest of your life.* If you are driving, listen to some good music, a news program you like, or an audiobook. If you are on the subway, train, or bus, or in a taxi, do the same, or take a nap, read, play games on your mobile phone, or watch a TV program or movie on your personal media player.

☞ *Set aside time for yourself.* In the transition between work and home (outside of your commute), do something by yourself. Taking a walk, going shopping, or getting something to drink at a coffee shop can help you decompress and take the edge off a long day.

☞ *Make sure that your leisure hours are for leisure activities.* Leave work at work and maximize your down time with activities that will help take you far way from the office.

In addition to these helpful ideas, here are a few common-sense things you can do to beat stress:

☞ *Get enough sleep.* Adequate sleep fuels your mind, as well as your body.

☞ *Eat a balanced, nutritious diet.* Eating several balanced, nutritious meals throughout the day will give you the energy to think rationally and clearly.

☞ *Reduce sugar and caffeine.* In excessive amounts, the temporary "highs" they provide often end in fatigue or a "crash" later.

☞ *Do not use alcohol or drugs to escape from the problem.* These will only mask the issue at hand. Instead, deal with the issue head on and with a clear mind.

☞ *Exercise regularly.* Find at least 30 minutes, three times per week, to do something physical. Nothing beats aerobic exercise to dissipate the excess energy.

Although you cannot eliminate stress completely, you can reduce and manage it. Figure out what works for you and make it a part of your daily routine.

E. Comprehension Check: Without looking back at the article, list some ways to help leave stress at the office.

F. Rethink: What can your company do to help reduce stress for its employees?

Section 4 ◆ Activity: Stress survey

Directions: Use the information in this unit to create a workplace stress survey. Follow these instructions and one of the examples below:

Steps

1. Decide what the focus of your survey will be.

2. With your focus in mind, write 10–15 stress-related questions or statements.

3. Determine how respondents will answer your questions (*i.e.,* 5-point scale or open answer).

4. Survey 10–12 people. Be sure to ask the respondents questions rather than just handing them your survey.

5. Compile results by tallying scores or noting the most common answer for each question and how many times it was given (in the form of a percentage).

6. Present results to the class.

Examples

Example 1

Focus: *Stress from people you work with*

5– Most of the time   4– Quite often   3– Sometimes   2– Rarely   1– Almost never

Do you get along well with your co-workers?	5	4	3	2	1
Do your co-workers frustrate or irritate you?	5	4	3	2	1
Are you ever jealous of your co-workers?	5	4	3	2	1

Example 2

Focus: *Stress from your job*

Open answer

1. What is the most stressful thing about your job? _____

2. What kind of stress do you feel most often from your job? _____

3. How do you reduce stress from your job? _____

Useful phrases   ⊙ CD 2 track 18, second part

What to say when you first approach someone

Pardon/Excuse me, I'm doing a survey on/about ___.

Would it be okay if I asked you a few questions?

Reporting results

The majority of the people ___.

Most people ___.

Quite a few people ___.

About half of the people ___.

Hardly any of the people ___.

Almost no one ___.

◆ Solving Problems ◆

Section 1 ◆ Starting Point: Problems

A. Warm Up: Discuss the following questions with a partner.

1. What have been some of the most challenging or difficult problems you have faced in your career? How about in your personal life? How did you overcome them?

2. What type of problems is your company, department, or team trying to deal with or overcome these days? In your opinion, what is the best way to tackle them?

3. What are some perennial challenges your company has faced over the years? What do you think are some potential solutions to these nagging problems?

B. Group Work: Below are three common types of problems in business and an example of each one. Work with another pair and come up with solutions for them.

The situation goes from bad to worse.

Example: Consumers in Country A are furious because they have just learned that beverages from a large, well-known soft drink company contain pesticides. The brand is quickly becoming a symbol of disrepute and blame, not to mention lawsuits. The biggest asset for the company, its reputation, is in danger, too. What can be done to address this problem and save the company's tarnished image?

The desired objective is not achieved within acceptable parameters (e.g., safety, quality, time, money).

Example: An electronics company's profits for the first quarter of the year were 10% lower than projected. What can they do to boost sales in the competitive mobile phone market?

Current understanding is insufficient, resulting in confusion or concern about the situation.

Example: Someone you have worked with for several years is being accused of a crime. He claims he is innocent of the charges. So far, however, the evidence to support either the accusation or your co-worker's claim is far from conclusive. The case could go either way. What do you think your company should do in this situation?

C. As a Class: Share your solutions to the problems above. Decide who came up with the best ideas.

Section 2 ♦ Communication Strategies: ⊙ CD 2 track 19
Dealing with problems

Part 1: Read, listen to, and say these sentences and phrases.

Analyzing

What exactly is the problem?
How serious is it?
Who's involved?
What/Who is affected by the situation?
Has this happened before?
How often is it happening?
How are we going to take care of/deal with this?
What should we do first?
Who's the best person to handle ___?
What stands in our way?
How much is this going to cost?
How risky is ___?
What are the consequences of ___?
How much time do we have?

Brainstorming

Can we spend a few minutes trying to come up with some ideas?
Let's take a few minutes to see what we can come up with.
We need to come up with some ideas.
Let's think about this.
Let's toss some ideas around.
Let's brainstorm some ideas.

Forecasting

What if we ___?
What if we didn't do anything (about ___)?
What's the worst thing that could happen?
What's the best possible outcome?
What's the most likely thing that will happen?
Do you (really) think that could/will happen?

Managing

How can we break this down?
There are two/three different ways we could ___.
We've narrowed it down to two/three possibilities.
There are only two/three ways to look at this.

Evaluating

Are things getting any better (or worse)?
Is there anything we could do/be doing better?

Part 2: Fill in the blanks with the phrases in **bold** type. When you are finished, read the dialogs with a partner. Then switch roles and read the dialogs again.

⊙ CD 2 track 20

Do you really think   What's the worst thing

Has that happened before   serious

What are we going to do   What do you mean

A: We got* a problem. Our earnings for this quarter are lower than expected.

B: How _____ is it?

A: It's worse than we first thought.

B: _____ by worse?

A: This is the third quarter in a row.

B: You're kidding! _____?

A: I'm sure we're going to have a meeting. It could get ugly.

B: Really? _____ that could happen?

A: Some people could get fired.

B: Fired? _____?

A: Yes. We lost a few people about three months ago over the same thing.

B: _____ that could happen again?

A: I'm sure the executives will give us an earful – and heads may roll.

* Informal spoken form of "we have got"

How much is this going to cost us   What exactly is the problem

What are the consequences   involved

A: I just heard that the company is being sued for consumer fraud.

B: Fraud? _____?

A: The suit claims that some people were charging retail customers for memberships in a discount program that had no real benefits.

B: I can't believe it! Who's _____?

A: Management is looking into it.

B: _____?

A: A lot. But actually, it really depends on whether or not the case goes to trial.

B: _____ if it does?

A: Not good, that's for sure!

break this down   come up with some ideas

Before leaping to conclusions   two ways to look at this

A: I can't believe a little disagreement turned into such a serious argument. That could cost us this deal.

B: I know. Well, can we spend a few minutes trying to _____
_____ about how to take care of this?

A: I think much of the responsibility falls on Laura and Jim. They should go
and apologize.

B: _____, we better* focus on what happened
and why it happened. So, how can we _____?

A: In my opinion, there are just _____ . . .

   * Informal spoken form of "had better"

Part 3: With a partner, create and practice a dialog based on a problem you are
currently dealing with at work, a work-related situation from the past, or one
that you create specifically for this task. Use as many business communication
strategies from this chapter as you can. When you are finished, practice your
dialog with your partner. Then perform it in front of the class.

Part 4: Form a group with another pair. Pretend that you work for the companies
below. Each one has a problem that needs to be resolved. Use communication
strategies from this chapter to help you act out each situation. The context is a
business meeting.

1. "Company 1" grew too quickly and its products and services flew out the door.
   But the company's infrastructure has not been able to keep up with the
   growth. New trained workers and new space are needed immediately. Its
   existing personnel, systems, and processes are simply unable to sustain the
   company's rapid expansion.

2. "Company 2" moved to additional products and services to drive its revenue.
   But managing the new revenue stream (cash flow, billing, payment methods,
   etc.) is not right for the company. It does not fit with the company's main effort
   and mission, and is a distraction to the whole organization. Now the company
   is mired in a mess of its own creation.

3. "Company 3" was once confident and proud of its own success. It had great
   products and a healthy bottom line, and grew steadily in a strong market. Over
   the years, however, it has lost market share to smaller, more innovative
   companies. Its revenues are down and its customer base has shrunk
   noticeably.

4. "Company 4" has a lot of well-qualified people working at the top of their game,
   but they are not aligned around a common goal. As a result, nobody at the
   company has a clear idea of who is doing what. There is a lot of overlap and
   redundancy, as well as a lot of gaps and things that fall through the cracks –
   all of which is hurting the bottom line.

Part 5: Wasting time is another common business problem. How do you waste time at work? Do you ever procrastinate? Below is a list of reasons why people put something off until another day or time. Put a "✔" next to each item that causes you to postpone doing what you should be doing.

1. Finding the task boring or unpleasant
2. Dealing with distractions (*e.g.,* personal problems, daydreaming, noise, *etc.*)
3. Feeling overwhelmed because of the difficulty or complexity of a task
4. Having difficulty prioritizing tasks (to include switching between them and only getting a little of each one done)
5. Fearing the consequences of failure (*i.e.,* you feel that it will be hard to complete the task according to expectations or an accepted standard)
6. Being a perfectionist (which causes you to devote too much time to certain parts of the task)
7. Feeling negatively toward the person who asked you to complete the task

Other(s): _____

What are some ways to effectively deal with procrastination at work? Brainstorm some ideas with your group, and write them in the box below.

```
┌─────────────────────────────────────────────────────┐
│                                                       │
│                                                       │
│                                                       │
│                                                       │
│                                                       │
│                                                       │
│                                                       │
│                                                       │
│                                                       │
│                                                       │
└─────────────────────────────────────────────────────┘
```

Now share your ideas with the class.

Section 3 ♦ Reading: Problem solving

Problem solving is the process of tackling problems in a systematic and rational way. It requires patience, understanding, and hard work. With the following exercises and article, you will have an opportunity to examine this issue and express your opinions about it.

A. Activate: Work with a partner. Match the strategies for handling conflict on the left with their definitions on the right.

1. ___ Accommodation   a. Address the issue but do not resolve it to the complete satisfaction of either party

2. ___ Avoidance   b. Strive for harmony by complying with the other party's needs

3. ___ Collaboration   c. Directly and forcefully work through differences

4. ___ Competition   d. Refrain from dealing with the conflict (to buy time or take a break)

5. ___ Compromise   e. Achieve goals together and improve the relationship between parties

6. ___ Confrontation   f. Be aggressive and use power to beat the other party

B. Discuss: Discuss these questions.

1. Which of these strategies do you think is the most effective overall? Why?

2. Which strategy do you tend to use most often? Why?

3. Can you think of situations where one strategy would work better than another one? Explain.

C. Focus: Below are some tips on how to improve your chances of successfully resolving conflicts. Some are helpful (✔) and others are not (✗). Reword the ones that are not to make them helpful.

1. ___ Argue over everything. Do not pick and choose your conflicts.

2. ___ Develop a reputation as someone who never admits when you are wrong.

3. ___ Do not knock down the ideas of others without having something else to suggest.

4. ___ If possible, let the other person speak first, to gain insight into what it takes to satisfy them.

5. ___ Exaggerate what you are saying instead of basing your statements on facts.

6. ___ Do not lose your temper.

7. ___ Use sarcasm or stinging humor to respond.

When trying to resolve conflicts, what do you need to do better? Explain by using some of the tips above.

D. Read: Read the following article.

Problems you face at work can be quite challenging, overwhelming, or complex. And finding the right solution, especially in a timely manner, is usually not an easy task. It almost always requires a great deal of understanding, patience, and hard work.

There are four basic **levels** of conflict:

Intrapersonal. This conflict is within an individual. It is rooted in one's ideas, attitudes, emotions, and values.

Interpersonal. This conflict is between individuals, including family members, friends, lovers, roommates, and co-workers.

Intragroup. This conflict is the result of clashing individual differences within a small group (*e.g.,* family, team members, or a committee).

Intergroup. This conflict is between groups (*e.g.,* labor and management, protestors and government, different nations), and is complicated because of the number of people involved and their histories.

For each level of conflict, there are four **stages**:

1. *Latent.* The conflict is dormant.
2. *Manifestation.* The conflict becomes overt.
3. *Escalation.* The conflict intensifies.
4. *Resolution.* The conflict settles.

Once a problem becomes overt, here is a series of **steps** you can take to help you deal with it:

1. Identify or state the problem.
2. Gather information about the problem.
3. Prioritize information gathered.
4. Develop a list of possible solutions to resolve the problem.
5. Evaluate practicality of proposed solutions.
6. Select the best solution and course of action.
7. Implement the solution.
8. Assess results.
9. Adjust future action(s).

E. Comprehension Check: **Without** looking back at the article, use the following prompts to help you summarize what you read.

Levels

(1) Within individuals –

(2) Between individuals –

(3) Within a group –

(4) Between groups –

Stages

(1) Dormant –

(2) Overt –

(3) Intensifies –

(4) Settles –

Steps

(1) Identify . . .

(2) Gather . . .

(3) Prioritize . . .

(4) Develop . . .

(5) Evaluate . . .

(6) Select . . .

(7) Implement . . .

(8) Assess . . .

(9) Adjust . . .

F. Rethink: What will you try to do the next time a problem arises where you work?

Section 4 ◆ Activity:
Problems in the news

Directions: As a class, make a list of some social, economic, and political problems in the news today. Write them in the box below.

Now choose three to five of these and, in pairs or groups, discuss how you would go about solving each one. When everyone is finished, share your ideas with each other. See where you agree or disagree, and then discuss the problems and solutions in more depth.

♦ Getting a Job: Résumé and Cover Letter ♦

Section 1 ♦ Starting Point: Jobs

A. Warm Up: Discuss the following questions in a group:

Part 1: How many different jobs have you had?
What's the best job you have ever had?
Among all of your friends, who has the best job? Why?

Part 2: When was the last time you applied for a job? What was the position?
What steps were involved in the application process?
What was the interview like?

Part 3: What type of personal qualities do you think most employers are looking for?
Make a list in the box below. Then circle all of the words that describe you.

hard-working positive attitude

What is your dream job? What skills do you need to have in order to do this job well?

Section 2 ♦ Communication Strategies: Résumé

A résumé is a written document that lists your work experience, skills, and educational background. It is used as a marketing tool for job seekers.

Task 1: Prepare to write a resumé

Switch books with a classmate and ask the following questions. Write their answers down on the lines below.

Step 1 – Contact information

What is your address? _____

What is your email address? _____

What is your telephone number (include area code)? _____

Step 2 – Career Objective

What kind of job do you want? Be specific.
[Use the two prompts and examples below to help you.]

♦ To obtain a/an ___ position at a/an ___ requiring ___ skills.

☞ To obtain an entry-level sales position at an advertising agency requiring excellent marketing skills.

☞ To obtain an administrative position at a large multinational corporation requiring strong leadership skills.

♦ ___ seeking a position at a/an ___to apply skills and experience in ___.

☞ Graphic designer seeking a position at Company A to apply skills and experience in web page design.

☞ Lawyer seeking a position at a New York law firm to apply skills and experience in trial law.

Your objective: _____

_____

* *Make sure that you tailor your objective to each employer you target/every job you seek.*

Step 3 – **Education**

What is your undergraduate college or university?

_____

List your postgraduate school(s) and degree(s) or area(s) of study.

_____

Write answers to the following questions – in this order – for each school on the lines above:

1. What is its name? Where is it located? [first line]
2. What is your degree or certificate? When did you receive it? [second line]

Example:

SIT Graduate Institute, Brattleboro, Vermont, USA
MS (Master of Science in Management, 2003)

Step 4 – **Work Experience**

Begin with your partner's current position and work in reverse chronological order. Use action words to list specific duties and responsibilities. When talking about current employment, be careful to use the present tense. This signals that your partner is still performing these tasks at their current job. When talking about past employers, use the past tense to signal that your partner is are no longer working for that company. Include answers to each question for every position:

1. What is/was your job title?
2. Where do/did you work?
3. Where is/was it located?
4. When did you work there? (*e.g.,* 2005–Present)
5. What are/were your job duties and responsibilities?

Example:

Marketing Manager, Company A, Osaka, Japan (2003–2006)
Directed three departments: Sales, Advertising, and Research. Developed new regional office in Kobe. Met weekly with advertising staff to supervise television, print, and Internet advertising. Supervised development of 100-page company catalogue. Directed sales research committee in client satisfaction survey and analysis. Coordinated annual trade show presence.

* *Notice that descriptions of job duties and responsibilities are not written in complete sentences. Each one starts with an* **action verb** *or* **adverb***.*

Current or most recent job

_____

_____

_____

_____

_____

_____

_____

Previous position 1

_____

_____

_____

_____

_____

_____

_____

Previous position 2

_____

_____

_____

_____

_____

_____

_____

Previous position 3

_____

_____

_____

_____

_____

_____

_____

* If they have more work experience than this, continue on a blank piece of paper.

Step 5 – Related Experience

Write your partner's answers to the following questions on the lines below.*
If your partner says "no" or "none," do not write anything.

1. Do you have any special skills or training?

2. What languages can you speak? At what level? Only list languages
   you speak at an intermediate level or higher, not ones that you are
   unable to hold a conversation in.

3. Have you ever done any volunteer work or community service?

_____

_____

_____

_____

_____

_____

_____

** You can list these as bulleted points under the heading "Related Experience"
on your résumé. This section follows "Work Experience."*

Task 2: Write a résumé

Return the textbook to your partner. Use the information in Task 1 to handwrite a résumé on a blank piece of paper. Follow the example layout below.

Full name
Home address
Email address, telephone number

Career Objective

To obtain a/an ___ position within/at a ___ requiring ___ skills.

Education

Postgraduate school name(s), location(s) (city, state/region, country)
Degree(s), year(s)

Undergraduate university or college, location (city, state/region, country)
Degree, year

Professional Experience

Current or most recent job title, Name of company/organization,
location (city, state/region, country), year(s)
Job duties and responsibilities

Previous job title, Name of company/organization,
location (city, state/region, country), year(s)
Job duties and responsibilities

Previous job title, Name of company/organization,
location (city, state/region, country), year(s)
Job duties and responsibilities

Previous job title, Name of company/organization,
location (city, state/region, country), year(s)
Job duties and responsibilities

Related Experience

- Special skills or training
- Languages
- Volunteer work or community service

References available upon request

Task 3: Assignment

Step 1

Use the example résumé, your handwritten notes, and the formatting rules below to help you type your first draft.

- ☞ Use Times New Roman font.

- ☞ **Bold** and **enlarge** (16 point) your name at the top.

- ☞ Your contact information should be 11pt regular.

- ☞ Font size for all headings should be **12pt**. Headings should be **bold** and Small Caps. All other text should be 11pt regular.

- ☞ **Bold** all **school names** and **job titles**.

- ☞ Use one line space between headings, schools, and jobs.

- ☞ Indent all information other than your headings.

- ☞ Keep all information in sections aligned.

- ☞ Bold "**References available upon request**."

Step 2

After receiving feedback from your teacher, make any necessary changes and type your final draft.

Section 3 ◆ Communication Strategies: Cover letter

A cover letter is a document sent with your résumé to provide additional information about your skills and experience, as well as reasons why you are interested in and qualified for the job you are applying for.

Task 1: Write a cover letter for your dream job

Follow the steps below to write a cover letter for a company you would like to work for and the position you would like to have.

Step 1 – Heading

1. Write today's date at the top.

2. After a line space, write the name of the person you are writing to (**not** "To Whom It May Concern") and the complete address.

   * *You may have to do some research to get this information.*

3. Write "Dear" followed by the recipient's title (*i.e.,* Mr., Ms., Dr.), the recipient's last name, and a colon.

Step 2 – First Paragraph *[Reasons why you are writing]*

☞ State your interest in the position you are applying for or say that you were referred by someone.

☞ Express that you are an excellent match for their needs.

Useful phrases

I am very interested in applying for the position of ____ (job title) at ____ (name of company) which was advertised in/on ____ (newspaper name/ website) on ____ (date).

I am very interested in working as a ____ (job title) for/at ____ (name of company/organization).

____ (person's name) informed me of a/an ____ (type of position) position that is available at your company.

____ (person's name) informed me that you are looking for someone with ____ (specialty) skills.

With my qualifications and experience, I believe I am an excellent match for your needs.

My experience/education/background/skills make(s) me an ideal candidate for the/this position.

Example

I am very interested in working as Marketing Manager at Company A. With my qualifications and experience, I believe I am an excellent match for your needs.

Practice below:

Step 3 – **Middle two paragraphs** *[what you have to offer]*

☞ Provide detail about your qualifications for the position.

☞ Stress your accomplishments and achievements rather than job duties and responsibilities.

☞ Expand on specific items from your résumé that are relevant to the job you are seeking.

☞ Show knowledge of the company.

☞ Tailor these paragraphs to the needs described in the job advertisement.

Useful phrases

First of all (To begin with), I have a ___ degree from ___.

I have (also) been a ___ for ___ years.

I have more than ___ years of ___ (type of) experience.

I have several years of experience as a ___.

For ___ (number) years, I have been ___.

Since ___ (year), I have ___.

During my career, I have ___.

I have strong ___ skills.

I have had several opportunities to ___.

According to your advertisement, this position requires ___ (skills). I developed these skills when ___.

As a/an ___ (current job) for ___ (company), I have ___.

I have helped/worked with/developed ___.

Prior to my current position, I was working for ___ (company), where I ___ (jobs, tasks, skills).

I have always had a strong interest in ___.

Your company has/is ___.

Example

First of all, I have a Master's degree in Business Communications from the University of Northern Asia. I have ten years of experience in the field of marketing, including three years at ABC Corporation. During my time there, I established a new international market in the Philippines and set up a regional office in Manila. I also supervised a new Internet advertising effort, resulting in a considerable increase in online sales.

Practice below:

Step 2 – Concluding paragraph(s)

☞ Express your desire for a job interview.

☞ Reiterate how you are a perfect fit for the job.

☞ Mention how they can get in touch with you.

☞ Say that you look forward to hearing from or meeting them.

☞ Thank them for the opportunity.

Useful phrases

I welcome the opportunity to discuss my qualifications with you.

I would appreciate the opportunity to interview for the position with you.

I am confident that I can perform the job effectively, and I am excited about the idea of working for your company/organization.

I am confident that I would be a great fit for your company/organization.

If you would like to schedule an interview, please call me at the number listed above.

You may reach me at the above phone number or email address.

I look forward to hearing back from you (to arrange an interview).

I look forward to hearing from you soon.

Thank you for your consideration.

Example

I am confident that with my qualifications and proven success, I would be a great fit for your company. I would appreciate an opportunity to interview for this position, and I can be reached at the email, telephone, and postal addresses on my résumé.

I look forward to hearing from you, and I thank you for your kind consideration.

Practice below:

Task 2: Type your cover letter

Use the template below to help handwrite (in class), then type (for homework), your cover letter. Make sure that you use the same size font (11pt) for your cover letter that you used for your résumé.

Your Street Address
City, State and Postal Code, Country
Telephone Number
Email Address

Month Day, Year

Mr./Ms./Dr. Full Name
Title
Name of Organization
Street or P. O. Box Address
City, State and Postal Code, Country

Dear Mr./Ms./Dr. Last Name:

I am very interested in applying for the position of Administrative Assistant at ABC Company which was advertised in the Daily Newspaper on Month date (*e.g.,* March 22). My qualifications and experience make me an ideal candidate for this position.

In addition to my extensive office experience, I have strong communication, customer service, and administrative skills. I have also . . .

Prior to my current position, I was working for XYZ Company, where I . . .

Thank you for your consideration. I look forward to hearing from you to arrange an interview.

Sincerely,

(Your handwritten signature)

Your full name typed

Enclosure(s)*

* If you are sending a résumé together with your cover letter, that is your "Enclosure." If you are sending more documents than this, make sure that you use the plural form, "Enclosures."

Task 3: Edit and revise

Step 1 – Check for common cover letter errors by answering the following questions.

Yes No

1. ☐ ☐ Did you tailor your cover letter specifically for the job you are applying for?

2. ☐ ☐ Did you convey a genuine interest in the position and a long-term pledge to fulfilling its duties?

3. ☐ ☐ Does every word of every sentence relate directly to your purpose for writing?

4. ☐ ☐ Have you reconsidered every statement in your cover letter to avoid any that could be interpreted in an unfavorable way?

5. ☐ ☐ Does your cover letter demonstrate knowledge of the employer's business?

6. ☐ ☐ Did you demonstrate what you could do for an employer – <u>not</u> what he or she can do for you?

7. ☐ ☐ Is the tone of your letter serious and professional from beginning to end?

8. ☐ ☐ Did you use the first person ("I") voice throughout your letter?

9. ☐ ☐ Did you verify the accuracy of any company information that you mention in your cover letter?

10. ☐ ☐ Do you sound determined – not desperate – in your cover letter?

11. ☐ ☐ Did you mistakenly emphasize your flaws rather than your strengths by confessing your shortcomings?

12. ☐ ☐ Did you misrepresent/lie about yourself, your qualifications, or your experience?

13. ☐ ☐ Did you include personal preferences or demands?

14. ☐ ☐ Did you include your age, weight, height, marital status, race, religion, or any other personal information that does not directly pertain to the position that you are applying for?

15. ☐ ☐ Did you include any irrelevant personal interests or hobbies?

16. ☐ ☐ Have you misspelled any words or made any typos?

17. ☐ ☐ Are there any grammar mistakes?

18. ☐ ☐ Did you use correction fluid or a pen to make any corrections?

19. ☐ ☐ Did you forget to sign your letter?

20. ☐ ☐ Did you use a paper color other than white?

Answers for numbers 1-10 should be "Yes." Answers for numbers 11-20 should be "No."

Step 2 – Make any necessary corrections and retype your cover letter.

Step 3 – After receiving feedback from your teacher, make any necessary changes and type your final draft.

◆ Getting a Job: Interview ◆

Section 1 ◆ Communication Strategies: Interview

Your résumé and cover letter only function as an entrance test to get a job interview. It is the interview itself that determines whether or not a potential employer will hire you. For this reason, it is the single most important part of landing your dream job.

Task 1: Gather facts before the interview

Part 1: What do you already know about the company you want to work for? You should know the following information. Put a ✔ next to the items you could intelligently talk about with your classmates right now.

1. ☐ Key people in the organization
2. ☐ Major products or services
3. ☐ Size in terms of sales and employees
4. ☐ Locations other than your community
5. ☐ Organizational structure of the company
6. ☐ Major competitors
7. ☐ View of the company by clients, suppliers, and competition
8. ☐ Latest news reports on the company or on local or national news that affects the company

For the boxes you did not check, do research on these items (for homework). It is vital that you know the company well and can speak confidently about it.

Perform this exercise each and every time before you have your interview. It will help reduce anxiety, as well as improve your chances of getting the job.

Part 2: In addition to knowing information about the company, you need to identify certain personal qualities in yourself that will portray you in a positive light to the interviewer. To practice doing this, tell a classmate, via specific examples, how you are:

☞ Adaptable	☞ Organized
☞ Analytical	☞ Productive
☞ Articulate	☞ Respectful
☞ Compassionate	☞ Responsible
☞ Creative	☞ Team-minded
☞ Decisive	☞ Tenacious
☞ Goal-oriented	☞ Trustworthy
☞ (a) Leader	

Task 2: Handle the job interview

Put a ✔ next to each thing you do or do not do (or are ready for) before, during, and after an interview. When you are finished, discuss why each one is important (for any interview you will have), what you need to work on, or any embarrassing experiences you may have had.

1. ☐ Dress appropriately for the position (as if you were working there).
2. ☐ Be sure you know exactly where the interview will be held and how long it takes to get there.
3. ☐ Arrive at the interview a few minutes early.
4. ☐ Be on your best behavior from the time you arrive at the company.
5. ☐ Do not smoke or chew gum.
6. ☐ Bring extra copies of your résumé, a pen, and a pocket calendar/notebook, and offer your business card if you have one.
7. ☐ Do not leave your cell phone on.
8. ☐ Be ready for small talk.
9. ☐ Do not use improper language, slang, or pause words (*e.g.,* "um," "uh," etc.)
10. ☐ Answer questions truthfully and in as much detail as necessary.
11. ☐ Stress your achievements and explain how your qualifications make you the best candidate for the position (*i.e.,* show how you can help the company or organization).
12. ☐ Show off the research you have done on the company and industry when responding to questions.
13. ☐ For a challenging question, ask for it to be repeated in order to give you a little more time to think about an answer.
14. ☐ Use body language and nonverbal feedback to show interest.
15. ☐ Do not speak badly about previous employers.
16. ☐ Substitute strengths for weaknesses (*i.e.,* transform any negatives into positives).
17. ☐ Close the interview by telling the interviewer(s) that you *want* the job and asking about the next step in the process.
18. ☐ Try to get a business card from each person you interviewed with.
19. ☐ Thank the interviewer.
20. ☐ Immediately take notes after the interview is concluded, so you do not forget crucial details.

Task 3: Answer common interview questions

When answering common interview questions:

1. Focus on work-related experience.
2. Provide lots of details.
3. Be specific and exact.
4. Talk about your qualifications for the job.
5. Show how the skills you do have relate to the job you are applying for.

With a partner, practice answering the following interview questions. Pretend you are interviewing for your dream job.

1. Tell me about yourself.
2. What type of position are you looking for?
3. What experience do you have in this field?

4. Why did you apply for this job? Why do you want to work for ___?

5. Why do you think you would do well at this job?

6. How long would you expect to work for us if hired?

7. Do you know anyone who works for us?

8. Are you applying for other jobs?

9. What do you know about our company/organization?

10. Can you tell me something about your current/previous job?

11. Why did you leave your last job?/Why do you want to leave your current job?

12. Have you ever been asked to leave a position?

13. What is your ideal job?

14. What are your career goals?

15. What do you see yourself doing five years from now?

16. What are your strengths? Weaknesses?

17. What would your co-workers say about you?

18. What are some of your most important career accomplishments?

19. Describe a difficult situation you had to deal with at work. How did you handle it?

20. What have you learned from mistakes on the job?

21. What qualities do you look for in a boss?

22. How would you describe your work ethic?

23. What motivates you to do your best on the job? How do you motivate others?

24. How well do you work under pressure?

25. How well do you adapt to new situations?

26. How well do you work with people? Do you prefer working alone or on teams?

27. Why should we hire you instead of other candidates for this position? What unique experience or qualifications separate you from them?

28. What are your salary requirements?

29. Are you willing to relocate?

30. What questions do you have for me?

When you are finished, share your answers with the class. Work with your teacher and classmates to strengthen how you respond to these questions.

Task 4: Asking the interviewer questions

Do not be afraid to ask the interviewer a few questions. In fact, you will most likely be prompted to do so. Here are some of the most common questions people ask about a position:

1. What are the duties of the position?

2. What types of skills are you looking for?

3. What type of training program do you have?

4. What are the opportunities for promotion/advancement?

5. What hours will I be working?

6. What is the salary range for this position?

7. What benefits are available/provided?

Make sure that you do not ask a question about information that was already given, unless you are following up on something the interviewer said.

Task 5: Mock interview

Hold mock interviews in front of the class. If you are watching, take notes and provide feedback to the interviewer and interviewee. Let them know what they are doing well and what they need to work on.

Section 2 ♦ Communication Strategy: Thank-you letters

You must write a thank-you letter as soon as possible after an interview. A thank-you letter shows the interviewer that you appreciated the opportunity to discuss your qualifications, and reinforces your interest in the position.

To write a thankyou letter, follow these steps:

1. Thank the interviewer(s) for their time.
   (If you want the job) State how you are convinced that this position is a good fit for both of you.

2. Express appreciation for the information that the interview(s) provided about the company.

3. Expand on your cover letter and state how you have the skills they are looking for.

4. Say you look forward to hearing from them again.

Your Street Address
City, State and Postal Code, Country
Telephone Number
Email Address

Month Day, Year

Mr./Ms./Dr. Full Name
Title
Name of Organization
Street or P. O. Box Address
City, State and Postal Code, Country

Dear Mr./Ms./Dr. Last Name:

Thank you for taking the time to discuss the Administrative Assistant position at ABC Company with me.

After meeting with you and observing the company's operations, I am further convinced that my background and skills coincide well with your needs.

I really appreciate that you went out of your way to acquaint me with the company. I feel I could learn a great deal from you.

In addition to my qualifications and experience, I will bring excellent work habits and judgment to this position. With the countless demands on your time, I am sure that you require people who can be trusted to carry out their responsibilities with minimal supervision.

I look forward to hearing from you concerning your hiring decision. Again, thank you for your time and consideration.

Sincerely,

(Your handwritten signature)

Your full name typed

Now practice writing a thank-you letter on a blank piece of paper (in class). For homework, you can type it and give it to your teacher for feedback.

Section 3 ♦ Communication Strategy: Success on the job

Once you have landed your dream job, you will want to make sure you keep it. Prove to be an asset rather than a liability from day one.

Below is a list of 10 things you want to make sure you do from the moment you show up to work. As a class, discuss how each one is advantageous for your new career. Explain by using examples. When you are finished, feel free to add to the list. Think about things specific to the country you are working in.

1. Be likeable.

2. Play for the team.

3. Network effectively.

4. Believe in yourself, have a "can-do" attitude, and take risks.

5. Make deadlines.

6. Do not conduct personal business on company time.

7. Avoid dating someone you work with.

8. Have goals and know how to reach them.

9. Project an image of competence, character, and commitment.

10. Watch what you say, where you say it, and to whom you say it.

Others

♦ Business Emailing ♦

Section 1 ♦ Starting Point: Communicating online

A. Warm Up: What is the best way for you to get your message across? Rank the following forms of communication from most effective (1) to least effective (6) where you work.

___ Voice-mail
___ Meeting face to face
___ Text messaging
___ Email
___ Telephone
___ Formal writing (*e.g.* letters and faxes)

Why did you rank them in this order?

B. Pair Work: Discuss the following questions with a partner.

Part 1

1. How often do you use the Internet? How many hours a day are you online?

2. What do you usually use the Internet for? What do you spend the most time doing?

3. How do you use the Internet at work?

Part 2

1. How often do you check your email?

2. How many emails do you receive every day?

3. How do you use email for work-related purposes?

C. As a Class: What is netiquette? Why is it important?

Section 2 ◆ Parts of an email

Directions: Match the different components of an email with their descriptions.

1. From: andrea.williams@company.com
2. To: scott.smith@company.com
3. Cc: mark.jones@company.com
4. Bcc: yolanda.adams@company.com
5. Subject: Flexible arrival times
6. Attachment: List of company employees

7. Font style: Font size: **B** *I* U̲

8. Dear Mr. Smith:

9. Thank you for getting back to me. As you know, starting Monday, employees who have obtained the consent of their section managers will have the option of coming to work at a time between the hours of 7:00 a.m. and 9:00 a.m. In keeping with this new policy, hour-long lunch breaks will be scheduled between 11:30 a.m. and 1:30 p.m. The workday will continue to end nine hours after it begins, so employees arriving at 7:00 a.m. will leave at 4:00 p.m. Once an employee and a section manager have agreed on an arrival time, the employee will be due at work at that time every day.

   If you have any questions about this new policy, please feel free to drop by the HR office anytime between 9:00 a.m. and 5:00 p.m. Monday to Friday. You can also reach me at ext. 2358.

10. I appreciate your attention and cooperation.

11. Best regards,

12. Andrea Williams
    Company Inc.
    Human Resources Manager

Write the numbers on the lines.

____ Closing
____ Where the email is being sent
____ Person/People who will receive a copy of the email without the recipient knowing
____ Ending/Concluding line (thanking and/or referring to future contact)
____ Files or documents sent separately but added to the message
____ Who is sending the email
____ Salutation
____ What the email is about
____ Body of email
____ Person/People who will receive a copy of the email
____ Formatting tools
____ Sender's name, company, and job title

Section 3 ♦ Reading: Email writing guidelines

A. Activate: Below are six main reasons why people write emails.

1. Convey information
2. Explain a situation
3. Request action
4. Seek information
5. Persuade
6. Reply to communication previously received

Which of these do you do most often at work? Do you send email for any other reasons not listed above? Discuss with a partner.

B. Focus: How do you write an effective email? In groups, make a list of tips and present your ideas to the class. Think about what people should do before, during, and after composing a message.

Before

During

After

Other

When you have finished reading the following article, compare your notes with the tips in the reading.

C. Read: Read the following tips for writing effective emails and compare it to what you wrote.

Email writing has become an essential part of modern communication, especially in business. To help you compose professional emails more effectively, follow the guidelines below:

Before composing

1. *Consider your purpose.* Email is not always the best or most effective form of communication to use. A telephone call, face-to-face meeting, or formal correspondence may be more appropriate.

2. *Think before you write.* Think about the people you are writing to. Make sure that you are sending a message that will be both clear and useful.

3. *Assume nothing is private or secure.* Email is like sending a postcard, not a private letter. It is a permanent record and can easily be forwarded or intercepted.

Composing

1. *Descriptive subject lines get attention.* A strong subject line that identifies the message content enables your reader to file and retrieve your message later. Good descriptive subject lines allow easy scanning for message content in mailboxes. In forwards and replies, if the email topic changes, change the subject line.

2. *Be clear about style – formal vs. informal.* Make sure that you use the appropriate language for the type of message you're sending.

3. *Use good structure and layout.* Reading from a computer screen is different from reading from paper. Keep your paragraphs concise, and place a blank line after each paragraph. This allows your reader to scan your message quickly.

4. *Create single subject messages whenever possible.* Multiple subject messages are confusing and could result in missed or neglected information.

5. *Get your most important points across quickly.* Place your most important information in the first paragraph. Put supporting details in subsequent paragraphs. Readers will often scan the first paragraph and make a judgment about the entire message based upon those first few lines.

6. *Limit sentence length.* Twenty words or two lines should be enough in most cases. Nobody likes to read excessively long or wordy sentences. Get to the point and stick to it.

7. *Use bullets or numbers and short paragraphs whenever possible.* The more succinct your message is, the more likely your email will be read, understood, and acted upon.

8. *Use active rather than passive voice when possible.* In sentences written in active voice, the subject performs the action (*e.g.,* Dr. Taylor will present his research.). In sentences written in passive voice, the subject receives the action (*e.g.,* Research will be presented by Dr. Taylor.).

9. *Write as you speak, but do not write as you chat.* Avoid using slang, idioms, trendy abbreviations, and expressions that might obscure meaning.

10. *Refrain from using difficult vocabulary and technical jargon.* There is no need to impress. Instead, keep your message simple and clear.

11. *DO NOT TYPE IN ALL CAPS!* IT LOOKS AS IF YOU ARE YELLING AT THE READERS! Remember, if you emphasize everything, you will have emphasized nothing.

12. *do not type in all lower case and watch your punctuation.* If you violate the rules of English punctuation and usage, you make it difficult for the reader to read and understand.

After composing

☞ *Always proofread your document before you send it. Do not rely on spellcheck or grammarcheck.* Use correct spelling, grammar, punctuation, and specific information (*e.g.,* dates and times). Carelessness makes a poor impression and can damage your professional credibility.

☞ *Be careful with formatting.* Remember that when you use formatting (such as the choice, style, and size of the font and the layout – centering, *etc.*) in your emails, the person you are sending to may not be able to see it, or may see different formatting from what you intended.

☞ *Take care with rich text and HTML format.* Be aware that when you send an email in rich text or HTML format, the recipient might only be able to receive plain-text emails.

☞ *Avoid attaching unnecessary files.* By sending large attachments you can annoy the intended receiver and, in some cases, bring down an email system. Wherever possible, cut and paste the contents of your attachment directly into the body of your email.

☞ *Make sure that you want to send the message.* If you say something, you can always deny that you said it, but if you write it, you may be held accountable for a long time.

Other

☞ ***Just as it is not polite to give out a person's telephone number without his or her knowledge, it is not polite to give out someone's email address.*** For instance, when you send an email message to 30 people and use Cc to address the message, all 30 people often see each other's email address. The same is true if you put all 30 addresses in the To line. When you use Bcc, each recipient sees only two addresses – theirs and yours.

☞ ***When you reply, decide whether you want to send your reply just to the person who wrote to you or to everyone in the To line and the Cc line.*** If you choose "Reply all," everyone except those who got a Bcc of the original message will see your reply. This can be embarassing. Always check to see who you are replying to.

☞ ***Use the Cc (Carbon Copy) function when you want everyone to know all the people you are sending your message to and what replies you get.*** This can be valuable at work when you want to share information quickly with your colleagues.

☞ ***Use Bcc (Blind Carbon Copies) when addressing a message that will go to a large group of people who do not necessarily know each other.*** Bcc protects people's privacy.

☞ ***Think about who you are sending an email to.*** These days everyone receives too many emails. Unnecessary messages are annoying. If only a few people really need to receive your message, direct it only to them.

☞ ***Keep your signature short (4 to 6 lines) and to the point.*** Separate it from the body of your email using two dashes and a space (*e.g.*, -- John Smith).

D. Comprehension: Read the tips only. Do this one section at a time. After each one, close your book and see how many tips you can remember. If you need help, have your partner use prompts to jog your memory (*e.g.*, "Consider your . . ." "Think before . . ." "Assume . . .").

E. Rethink: Why is it so important to follow these guidelines when composing messages?

Section 4 ♦ Communication Strategies: Language for emails

Part 1: Read and say these sentences.

Salutations

Hello/Hi (semi-formal)
Dear Dr./Mr./Mrs./Ms. [last name] (formal)

Thanking

Thank you for getting back to me.
Thank you for ___.

Apologizing

I apologize for not getting back to you sooner/yesterday, but I ___.

I'm sorry for the delay in getting back to you. I've been out of the office./I've been away this week.

Referring to attachments

Please find attached ___.
I have attached the ___ below.
I received your email, but I cannot open the attachment.

Reason for message

I am writing to you (because) ___.
The reason I am sending this email/message is ___.

Inquiring

I would like to know ___.
Could you tell/send/mail me ___?

Responding to inquiries

With reference to ___./Regarding your inquiry ___.
As requested, I am sending you ___.

Offering assistance

Please let me know if I can be of any assistance.
If I can be of any assistance, please let me know.

Showing appreciation for assistance

Any information you could give would be helpful.
We appreciate anything you are able to do.

Requesting

Please take a look at ___ and let me know what you think.
Please look it over and get back to me at your earliest convenience.

Responding to requests

I will take a look at it when/after I ___.
I will look it over and get back to you as soon as I can.

Ending line

I look forward to hearing from you (soon).
I look forward to meeting/seeing you ___.
Please feel free to ___.
If you need anything (else), just let me know.

Closing

Best regards/Best wishes/All the best (semi-formal)
Sincerely (formal)

Part 2: Look at the following email and identify the communication strategies used. Write the strategy in the parentheses. Follow the example.

Font style: Font size: **B** *I* U̲

Dear Ms. Thornton [**Salutation**],

Thank you for [_____] the recent opportunity of serving you in the Loan Department. I am writing to you today [_____] to tell you about a new item we are providing valued customers like yourself to make it easier for them to do their banking with us. It is called "EZ Loan." All you have to do is print out one of the forms I have attached below [_____] anytime you need to make a payment. This will save you the trouble of coming down to the bank to pick up forms.

Let us know if we [_____] can be of assistance to you in any of the other numerous banking services that we offer, including checking accounts, savings accounts, and investment counseling.

Feel free to [_____] stop by the bank at any time during the week to discuss your further needs with our staff.

Sincerely [_____],

Frank Mitchell
Statewide Bank
Branch Manager

Part 3: Fill in the blanks with communication strategies in **bold** type.

a small token of our appreciation   I feel moved   Sincerely
Thank you for   Please accept the attached certificate

Dear Ms. Davis,

_____ your kind letter regarding your exceptional treatment by one of our employees. A copy of your letter has been forwarded to the personnel department and will be included in the employee's file.

So seldom is it that a customer takes the time to write a letter of appreciation, that _____ to reward your initiative.

_____, which, when presented, will entitle the bearer to a ten-percent discount on the merchandise being purchased at that time.

This is but _____ for customers like yourself who have helped us grow and prosper in this highly competitive marketplace.

Again, on behalf of our entire organization, I would like to extend you a heartfelt thank you.

_____,

Alejandro Lopez
Store Manager

Part 4: Write two emails. Follow the directions for each one below. Be sure to use communication strategies, as well as follow the tips given in the reading.

Email 1

Inquiry.   An inquiry email is a request for information that the writer believes the reader can provide. Regardless of its subject, the objective is to get the reader to respond with an action that satisfies the inquiry. Your task is to write an email inquiring about a product or service your company provides. Pretend you are a customer – not an employee. Here are some suggestions for organizing your letter, along with some example phrases.

> ***Paragraph 1*** – Identify yourself and, if necessary, your position, and your institution or firm.
> *I am a ___ at ___, a ___ (type of company).*

> ***Paragraph 2*** – Briefly explain why you are writing and how you will use the requested information.
> *My team is considering your ___. If we decide to ___, we will need ___.*

> ***Paragraph 3*** – List the specific information you need. You can phrase your requests as questions or as a list of specific items of information.
> *We have read/seen your ___ and we are very interested in ___.*

> ***Paragraph 4*** – Conclude your letter by offering your reader some incentive to respond.
> *I would be happy to talk to you further about your product/service.*

Email 2

Response.   A response email provides the answers or information requested in a letter of inquiry. The objective is to satisfy the reader with an action that fulfills their request. Your task is to respond to the inquiry letter written by one of your classmates. Here are some suggestions for organizing your letter, along with some example phrases.

> ***Paragraph 1*** – Express appreciation for requesting information about your product or service and refer to the inquiry.
> *Thank you for expressing interest in ___.*

> ***Paragraph 2*** – State what you are able to do. Itemize as necessary.
> *We can offer/provide ___.*

> ***Paragraph 3*** – Note any attachments you are including.
> *Attached you will find ___.*

> ***Paragraph 4*** – Conclude your letter by restating your appreciation and offering assistance.
> *Again, we appreciate your interest in ___. If you need further assistance, ___.*
> *We look forward to serving you again.*

◆ **Traveling** ◆

Section 1 ◆ Starting Point: Travel

A. Warm Up: Discuss the following questions in small groups.

1. How often do you get a chance to travel?
2. What countries have you visited?
3. What do you like about traveling? What do you dislike?
4. What are some of the benefits of traveling?
5. What do you like to know about a country before you travel there?
6. What place have you enjoyed traveling in the most? Where did you have the most fun?

7. What countries would you like to visit some day?
8. Have you ever been in a difficult situation while traveling?
9. Do you usually travel light?
10. What are some things you always take on a trip?
11. What is the best hotel you have ever been in or stayed at? What is the best airline you have ever flown on?
12. Do you enjoy buying souvenirs?
13. What do you usually eat when you travel abroad? In other words, do you try local cuisine or do you prefer to eat what you know (*e.g.* fast food or food from your country)?
14. Which country that you have been to has the best local cuisine?
15. How do you feel about tipping? Are you a generous tipper? Why or why not?

B. Group Work: Use the following elements of cross-cultural communication to compare two countries you know (*e.g.,* United States and Japan).

➤ *Greeting.* Bow, handshake, kiss on the cheek, or another way?

➤ *Eye contact.* Maintain or tend to avoid?

➤ *Body language.* Expressive or more reserved?

➤ *Personal space.* Close or more distant?

➤ *Physical contact.* Comfort or discomfort with touching?

➤ *Names.* First, last, or other?

➤ *Age.* Respect for elders?

➤ *Time.* Flexible or punctual?

➤ *Meal times.* Early or late?

➤ *Work time vs. personal time.* What seems to be valued more?

➤ *Gender roles.* Equal status between men and women?

➤ *Dating.* Are interracial (or international) relationships accepted?

➤ *Stereotypes.* What are some misconceptions that need to be debunked?

➤ *Ethnocentrism.* How prevalent is this?

➤ *Personal connections.* How important are these?

C. As a Class: Share your comparisons with your classmates. In doing so, notice the similarities and differences between countries.

Section 2 ◆ Communication Strategies: The language of traveling

⊙ CD 2 track 21

Part 1: Read, listen to, and say these sentences and phrases.

Travel/Airline Agent

Helping a customer book a flight

Where would you like to go?

When would you like to go?

What days would you like to travel?

One-way or round-trip?

Aisle or window seat?

Are you a member of our frequent-flyer program?

Do you have your frequent-flyer number?

How would you like to pay for your tickets?

Requesting a flight

How much is coach/business class/first class?

Would it be cheaper if I left on ___?

Is it direct/nonstop?

Is there a layover?

How long is the layover?

Do I have to change planes?

How much carry-on luggage am I allowed?

Is there a charge for luggage?

When does the next flight leave?

Are there seats still available?

Are there tickets available on standby?

What's the departure/arrival time?

Will I be able to make my connection?

Can I change my itinerary?

Has the flight been delayed?

*With minor adaptations, these sentences can be used with an airline agent over the phone, at a ticket counter, or with a travel agent.

Part 2: With a partner, create and practice a dialog based on the following flow chart. Use business communication strategies from this chapter to help you. When you are finished, switch roles. Create and practice a similar dialog **without** using the flow chart.

Situation: Asking about a flight and booking it

A1: (*Agent*) "Can I help you?"

B1: (*Customer*) Say that you're interested in making a reservation for a flight.

A2: Ask where they would like to go.

B2: Respond to your partner.

A3: Ask if they want a one-way or round-trip ticket.

B3: Say you want round-trip.

A4: Ask when they would like to depart and return.

B4: Respond to your partner. Then inquire about the price difference between coach and business class.

A5: Respond to your partner.

B5: Say that you're fine with coach (and that business class is too expensive). Then ask if the ticket would be cheaper if you left on a certain day or time.

A6: Ask if your partner is flexible with days and times.

B6: Respond affirmatively.

A7: Ask if your partner prefers a window or aisle seat.

B7: Respond to your partner. Then ask if it is a direct flight.

A8: Respond by saying there is a layover.

B8: Ask how long the layover is.

A9: Respond to your partner.

B9: Ask if you have to change planes.

A10: Respond affirmatively.

B10: Ask how much luggage you're allowed and if there is a charge.

A11: Respond to your partner. Then ask
if they are a frequent-flyer member.

B11: Respond affirmatively.

A12: Ask what the frequent-flyer
number is.

B12: Give them your number.

A13: Ask your partner how they would
like to pay for the ticket.

B13: Respond to your partner by
saying you'll pay with a credit card.

A14: Ask your partner for their
number and expiration date
and give them the ticket.

B14: Thank your partner for their assistance.

A15: Respond to your partner and
wish them a pleasant flight.

B15: Respond to your partner
and say goodbye.

Part 3: Read, listen to, and say these sentences and phrases.

Hotels

⊙ CD 2 track 22

Asking about a hotel room

Where are you staying?

How's your hotel/room?

How do you like it there?

Is everything okay at your hotel?

Checking a guest in

Do you have a reservation?

How many people?

How many nights will you be staying?

Would you like a smoking or nonsmoking room?

Would you like a room with a view of ____?

Do you need help with your luggage?

Arriving at a hotel

Do you have any vacancies/rooms available?

What are the rates?

Can I reserve/book a room?

Do you have a reservation for _____?

Do you have a room with two double beds?

Do you have room service/a pool?

What time is checkout?

Is there a penalty for late checkout?

Asking for assistance

Could you recommend a good restaurant?

Where can I exchange money?

Where can I buy ____?

Is there a/an _____ close by/nearby?

Is there a good place to ____ around here?

Where's the nearest _____?

How do I get to _____ (from here)?

What's the best way to get to _____ (from here)?

Part 2: With a partner, create and practice a dialog based on the following flow chart. Use business communication strategies from this chapter to help you. When you are finished, switch roles. Create and practice a similar dialog *without* using the flow chart.

Situation 1: Checking in at a hotel

A1: (*Guest*) Inquire about vacancies.

B1: (*Hotel clerk*) Say that there are rooms available. Then ask for how many people.

A2: Respond to your partner. Then ask what the rates are.

B2: Respond by asking what type of room they would like.

A3: Respond to your partner.

B3: Ask how many nights they will be staying.

A4: Respond to your partner.

B4: Give rates for those nights. Then ask if they want a smoking or nonsmoking room.

A5: Respond to your partner.

B5: Ask if they want a room with a view.

A6: Respond to your partner. Then ask about a pool and room service.

B6: Respond to your partner. Then ask how your partner would like to pay for the room.

A7: Respond to your partner by saying you'll pay with a credit card.

B7: Ask for their signature. Then ask if they need help with their luggage.

A8: Respond affirmatively.

B8: Say that you will have someone take them to their room.

A9: Ask what time checkout is.

B9: Respond to your partner.

A10: Ask if there is a penalty for late checkout.

B10: Respond to your partner.

A11: Thank your partner for their assistance.

B11: Respond to your partner and wish them a pleasant stay.

Situation 2: Asking for assistance at a hotel

A1: (*Guest*) Ask for a restaurant recommendation for lunch.

B1: (*Hotel clerk*) Ask what kind of food they want and how much they would like to spend.

A2: Respond to your partner.

B2: Tell your partner about a nice restaurant and how to get there (*i.e.*, around the corner and down the street on the left).

A3: Express appreciation. Then ask where you can exchange some money.

B3: Say that it's possible at the hotel. Then ask if they want to exchange money.

A4: Respond by saying that you will tomorrow morning. Then ask if there is a department store nearby. Say that you would like to go shopping after lunch.

B4: Say that there is one three blocks down from the restaurant on the same side of the street.

A5: Respond to your partner. Then ask where the nearest subway stop is.

B5: Give the cross streets.

A6: Say that you don't know where those streets are. Ask for the best way to get there from the department store.

B6: Give directions (*i.e.*, two blocks over and one block up).

A7: Express appreciation for their help.

B7: Respond to your partner. Then give them a hotel business card with contact information. Say to call if they get lost.

A8: Express appreciation and say goodbye.

B8: Respond to your partner.

Part 5: Read, listen to, and say these sentences and phrases.

Sightseeing and shopping

⊙ CD 2 track 23

Sightseeing

What would you like to do while you're here?
Where would you like to go while you're here?
Have you had a chance to look around?
What do you think of ___ so far?
Have you (ever) been to/seen/tried ___?
Would you like to go/see/try ___?
I can show you/take you to ___ (if you want/have time).
Will you have any time to ___?
If you have time, you should go to ___.
How about going to/doing/trying ___?
Why don't we (go to) ___?

Shopping – Shopper to salesperson

When do you open/close?
What are your hours?
Are you open on weekends?
Do you have this in a larger/smaller size?
Do you have something a little less expensive?
Do you have this/these in stock?
Do you have any more of these?
Where can I try this on?
Is this on sale?
Can/May I get it/this gift wrapped?

Shopping – Salesperson to shopper

May/Can I help you?
Can I help you find something?
Can I show you something?
Are you being helped?
Is someone helping you?
Is there anything I can help you with today?
Are you looking for something in particular?
Do you have anything in mind?
What size do you need?
Do you need anything to go with that?
Is there anything else I can interest you in?
Is there anything else I can help you with?
How would you like to pay for this?
Will that be cash or charge?

Part 6: With a partner, create and practice a dialog based on the following flow chart. Use business communication strategies from this chapter to help you. When you are finished, switch roles. Create and practice a similar dialog *without* using the flow chart.

Situation 1: Talking about what sights to see

A1: (*Host*) Ask what your partner would like to do while she or he is in ___ (city).

　　　　　B1: (*Guest*) Respond to your partner.

A2: Ask if your partner has had a chance to look around yet.

　　　　　B2: Respond affirmatively – a little.

A3: Ask your partner what she or he thinks of ___ so far.

　　　　　B3: Respond to your partner.

A4: Ask your partner if she or he has ever tried ___ food.

　　　　　B4: Respond to your partner (and say whether you like or dislike it).

A5: Ask your partner if she or he would like to go to ___ (place).

　　　　　B5: Respond to your partner.

A6: Ask if your partner will have time to take a short trip outside the city.

　　　　　B6: Say that you'd like to but you don't have time.

A7: Suggest one or two more things to do.

　　　　　B7: Respond to your partner.

A8: Tell your partner that you two should get going.

　　　　　B8: Respond to your partner.

Situation 2: Shopping for clothes

A1: (*Salesperson*) Ask if your partner needs any assistance.

B1: (*Shopper*) Say that you are looking for a jacket.

A2: Ask if they are looking for anything in particular.

B2: Respond to your partner.

A3: Show your partner some jackets and ask what size they need.

B3: Respond to your partner. Then ask if you can try one of the jackets on.

A4: Escort your partner to the fitting room.

B4: Ask if the jacket is on sale.

A5: Respond affirmatively. Then ask if they need anything to go with the jacket (*e.g.,* sweater, pants, *etc.*).

B5: Say that you only want to buy a jacket – and that you will take the one you tried on.

A6: Ask if they need any more assistance.

B6: Say, "No, thank you."

A7: Escort your partner to the cash register. Then ask how they would like to pay for the jacket.

B7: Say, "Cash." Then ask to have it gift wrapped (say it is for your brother/sister).

A8: Respond to your partner. Then give them the shopping bag.

B8: Thank your partner for their assistance.

Part 7: Read, listen to, and say these sentences and phrases.

Restaurants

⊙ CD 2 track 24

Common questions – Host and server to patron*

Do you have a reservation?

How many are in your party?

Are you waiting for someone?

Will someone be joining you?

May I put you on the waiting list for about five minutes?

Would you like to see the menu?

Can I get you something to drink?

Are you ready to order?

Is this all on one check or separate checks?

Is everything all right/OK?

Is there anything (else) I can get for you?

Would you care for dessert?

*You will find that these terms vary around the world. A *host* is also called a *Maître d'* or *headwaiter*. A *server* is also called a *waiter*. A *patron* is also called a *customer*. The feminine forms *hostess* and *waitress* have become less common.

Conversation with a friend

So, what are you in the mood for?

That sounds good.

I think I'll try _____.

How about an appetizer?

Why don't we share _____?

What would you like to drink?

Should we get a bottle of wine?

Are you ready to order?

Not yet. Give me another minute.

I haven't made up my mind.

What about dessert?

Shall we ask for the check?

It's on me this time.

Common questions – Patron to server

What is the special today?

What's good today?

What comes with that?

Does that come with _____?

What kind of dressing do you have?

Do you have a wine list?

Does this have any _____ (in it)?

May/Can/Could I have some more _____, please?

Where's the restroom?

Could I have the check?

Do I pay you or the cashier?

Can I have a receipt, please?

Part 8: With a partner, create and practice a dialog based on the following flow chart. Use business communication strategies from this chapter to help you. When you are finished, switch roles. Create and practice a similar dialog *without* using the flow chart.

Situation 1: Looking at a menu in a _____ restaurant

A1: Ask your partner what they want for dinner.

B1: Say that it is hard to decide. Then ask your partner what sounds good.

A2: Say that a couple of things caught your eye (*e.g.*, steak, pasta, *etc.*).

B2: Say that those do sound good.

A3: Ask your partner if they want to share an appetizer.

B3: Respond affirmatively. Then ask which one.

A4: Respond to your partner. Then say that you had better make up your mind about what main dish to order.

B4: Ask what your partner is going to have.

A5: Respond to your partner. Then ask what your partner will have.

B5: Respond to your partner. Then say you will have _____ to drink.

A6: Say that you will have one too.

B6: Respond to your partner. Then call the waiter or waitress over to your table.

Situation 2: Taking an order

A1: (*Host*) Ask if your partner
    has a reservation.

B1: (*Patron*) Respond affirmatively
    – give your last name

A2: Ask how many people are in
    his or her party.

B2: Respond to your partner.

A3: Ask them to follow you and escort
    your partner to their table
    (*e.g.,* "Right this way, please"). Then
    ask if your partner would like
    something to drink.

B3: Respond to your partner.

A4: Say that the waiter or waitress will
    be here shortly to take their order.

B4: Respond to your partner.

A5: (*Server*) Ask your partner if
    they are ready to order.

B5: Say that you'll have the ____.
    Then ask what comes with that.

A6: Say that it comes with a salad.

B6: Ask what kind of dressing they have.

A7: Respond to your partner. Then
    ask what they want to drink.

B7: Respond to your partner.

A8: Ask if your partner wants
    anything else.

B8: Say not right now. Then ask where
    the rest room is.

A9: (*Later*) Ask if everything was okay.

B9: Say that it was. Then ask for the
    check.

A10: Return to the table with the check.

B10: Ask if you pay them or if you just
     go up to the cashier.

A11: Say "the cashier." Then thank them
     for dining at your restaurant.
     Wish them a pleasant evening.

B11: Respond to your partner.

Part 9: Read, listen to, and say theses sentences and phrases.   ⊙ CD 2 track 25

Plans

Evening plans

Is there anything going on tonight?

What's going on tonight?

What do you want to do tonight?

What are you up for (tonight)?

What are you in the mood for?

What sounds like fun?

Parting

That was a lot of fun!

I had a great time.

Thanks for inviting me.

Let's do it again sometime.

Do you have my (cell) phone number/email address?

Do you have a business card?

Here's my business card.

I don't have a card on me right now.

You can reach me at _____.

Give me a call next time you're in.

I look forward to seeing you (again) next week/month.

Stay/Keep in touch.

Making plans

Are you free sometime next week?

How about next _____?

What about _____?

When would be good for you?

What would work for you?

Is ____ convenient for you?

Part 10: With a partner, create and practice a dialog based on the following flow chart. Use business communication strategies from this chapter to help you. When you are finished, switch roles. Create and practice a similar dialog *without* using the flow chart.

Situation: An evening out

A1: Ask your partner if there is anything going on tonight.

      B1: Say that you don't know.

A2: Ask your partner what they would like to do tonight – what sounds fun.

      B2: Respond to your partner.

A3: Say that what your partner wants to do does sound fun.

      B3: Suggest that you get going.

A4: (*Later*) Tell your partner that you had a great time.

      B4: Say that the two of you should do it again sometime.

A5: Agree with your partner.

      B5: Ask your partner for their phone number.

A6: Exchange phone numbers with your partner.

      B6: Ask your partner if they are free next weekend.

A7: Respond affirmatively.

      B7: Make a plan to meet.

A8: Respond to your partner.

      B8: Say you will call your partner in the next couple of days.

A9: Respond to your partner.

◆ Business Terms ◆

Books by David and Peggy Dustin Kehe

Basic Conversation Strategies — Through 12 units, high-beginner to low-intermediate students are taught to listen and reply appropriately using rejoinders, tag questions, clarification questions, and small talk, all basic skills needed to interact in English in everyday situations. The listening activities are designed to make students depend on their ears; they are best used with the two dramatically read dialogs on two audio CDs.

Conversation Strategies — 24 structured pair activities for developing strategic conversation skills at the intermediate level. Students learn the words, phrases, and conventions used by native speakers in active, give-and-take, everyday conversation.

Discussion Strategies — Carefully structured pair and small-group work at the advanced-intermediate level. Excellent preparation for students who will participate in academic or professional work that requires effective participation in discussion and seminars.

The Grammar Review Book — The grammar is based on the fossilized errors made by many people who have learned English by ear, often called generation 1.5. The students are often fluent in English and have large vocabularies, but they speak and write "street English," which limits their possible success in education and business.

Write after Input — A low-intermediate text teaching students to develop good paragraphs and short compositions. The listening and reading input is used for modeling and to provide topics the class can work on in common. Appropriate structure and style are a major focus of the exercises.

Writing Strategies: A Student-Centered Approach — Two texts jam-packed with writing activities. Each covers four modes of writing. Book One *(High Intermediate)* teaches • Description, • Narration, • Exposition, and • Comparison and Contrast. Book Two *(Advanced)* covers • Process, • Cause and Effect, • Extended Definition, and • Argumentation. Coordinated with these lessons are Fluency Writing Exercises and lessons on Grammar Problems and Terminology.

The Idiom Book — 1010 American idioms in 101 two-page lessons. Each idiom is presented in four contexts: a dialog, a reading (letter or email), matching idioms with definitions, and a paraphrasing activity. The dialog and reading are available on two audio CDs for listening and pronunciation.

The Modal Book — 14 units explore the form, meaning, and use of the American English modal verb system, one semantic grouping at a time.

A Phrasal Verb Affair — over 200 phrasal verbs are presented and practiced in the context of a 15-episode soap opera. A dramatic reading on CD is available.

Shenanigames — Grammar-focused, interactive ESL activities and games provide practice with a full range of grammar structures. Photocopyable.

Getting a Fix on Vocabulary — A student text and workbook that focuses on affixation—building words by adding prefixes and suffixes to a root.

Lexicarry — Pictures for Learning Languages the Active Way. Over 4500 everyday words and expressions in 192 contexts that make conversation and interactive learning easy.

Web Store: www.ProLinguaAssociates.com